D0553440

WITHDRAWN

QUICK PINT
AFTER WORK

QUICK PINT AFTER WORK

Luke Lewis

Illustrated by Shitty Watercolour

sphere

SPHERE

First published in Great Britain in 2014 by Sphere

ISBN 978-0-7515-5773-2

Typeset in Caslon by M Rules
Printed and bound in Great Britain by
Clays Ltd, St Ives plc

Papers used by Sphere are from well-managed
forests and other responsible sources.

Sphere
An imprint of
Little, Brown Book Group
100 Victoria Embankment
London EC4Y 0DY

An Hachette UK Company
www.hachette.co.uk

www.littlebrown.co.uk

For The Wriggler

Contents

Contents

Food and Drink

Relationships

The Media

Critics

At work

Modern life is rubbish

Foreword

Why is life so relentlessly awkward? What is the strange cosmic force that makes us stop dead in the middle of the street, clammy with shame upon remembering that time six weeks ago when we went in for a hug only for the other person to offer a handshake? Must we spend the rest of our lives turning over in our minds that incident where we introduced ourselves to an auditorium full of besuited delegates as a 'Webshite Editor' (this *has* happened to everyone, right?)? Why is the universe seemingly so fine-tuned for embarrassment? The answer, surely, is that we are forced to share it with other people. And other people are awful.

I'm convinced that any normal person, given the choice, would happily live his/her entire life in the psychic mode of a commuter: silent, solitary, troubled by no social obligations beyond occasionally sighing at the announcements, or tutting at the pushy git who asks everyone to move down the carriage. This is the natural karmic state of a British person, and secretly we all cherish it. Unfortunately, every commute must come to an end, and once we are cruelly ejected at either terminal – whether at home, or at work – we find that we are expected to actually talk to people. Sometimes for entire minutes on end. In meetings, over coffee, during dinner, to family, to colleagues. It is never-ending, and it is intolerable.

And there is always the lurking terror, with all this talking going on, that you might actually let slip how you feel about something. This cannot be allowed to happen. I mean, we're not French. Thankfully, British people have devised a brilliant way to ensure we never have to unburden ourselves emotionally, which is this: we *never actually say what we mean*. It is a wonderfully effective strategy, one that has served us well for centuries. Between cliché, office jargon, tabloidese, internet speak and general polite mumbling, what comes out of our mouths bears absolutely no relation to the truth. And that's fine. We like it that way. Consider that Britain leads the world in just two industries: financial services and PR. We are global leaders in bullshit. It's what we're good at.

Perhaps I'm more sensitive to this state of affairs than the average person. As the UK Editor of BuzzFeed, I spend every waking hour immersed in the internet. I think in lists. At night, I dream of memes. I am no longer capable of experiencing human emotion without reflexively running through a mental rolodex of sassy reaction GIFs. The internet is where I live. And as we all know, the internet, for all its transformative and liberating qualities, is the greatest mechanism ever devised for amplifying bullshit. Hoaxes go viral every day. Specifically, the verbal obfuscations that litter British life are turbo-charged by social media, where cliché and self-promotion are the dominant forms of expression.

Whether it's the Twitter user who describes himself as a 'social-media ninja' in his bio (translation: he once got retweeted by Caitlin Moran); the over-excitable teen who appends every Facebook status with 'YOLO!' (translation: she has just consumed a can of Monster energy drink on a school night); the self-conscious corporate type who puts a #hashtag #in #front #of #every #word (translation: he doesn't know how any of this actually works) … none of these people really mean what they say. Each one is using language as a means of performing a role. They're expressing a version of themselves, but it's not the *real* them.

You can see this phenomenon play out in all areas of life. Walk into a newsagent and survey the shelves groaning with magazines, each promising an 'exclusive' interview with the same celebrity. Meanwhile the news is little more than a succession of rote phrases, from the 'high-speed car chase' (as opposed to a slow one) to the 'frenzied knife attack' (as opposed to a gentle one), to the 'bosses' who are perennially 'holed-up for crunch talks' (translation: some men in suits are at a conference). Even the way we talk about weather is prone to this sort of distortion. If you ever hear it said of an event, 'The rain failed to dampen anyone's spirits', you can be absolutely certain that it pissed it down and everyone was miserable. Everything is a lie, even if it is a thoroughly well-meaning, British sort of a lie.

I'd been carrying all this in my head for years, but the moment of revelation came at work one afternoon when I found myself calling a meeting and saying by way of introduction, 'In this brainstorm, there are no bad ideas'. Which was, of course, pure, glaring bollocks. Most brainstorms are nothing *but* bad ideas. So why say it? One answer is that I am

4

quite possibly becoming a bit of a corporate douchebag. Another, kinder answer is that I am just as helplessly adrift in a world of hollow cliché as anyone else. But the episode made me think: what if there was a way to scythe through this linguistic piffle? What if you were to write a phrase book that translated all the bullshit into plain English? Could it be done?

My first attempt was a BuzzFeed article, 'What People Say At Work vs. What They Mean: 88 office clichés, translated'. It did pretty well, winning several hundred thousand views. The follow-up, 'What Londoners Say vs. What They Mean,' did even better: nearly a million views. People shared these articles with an enthusiasm that suggested they hadn't just found them vaguely amusing, they'd actually found them strangely cathartic. A publisher asked me if I'd like to write an entire book's worth. I said, 'Sounds great!' (translation: 'Sounds absolutely terrifying!') And here it is. I hope you like it. If you do, perhaps you might like to go on Amazon and leave a review, something original like, 'A real page-turner' (translation: 'I flicked through it without reading a word'), 'Uproariously funny' ('I smiled a couple of times'), or 'I couldn't put it down' ('I had to spend this stupid voucher on something').

THE AGONY OF
BEING BRITISH

What British people say, vs. what they mean

'**Whose round is it?**': I know exactly whose round it is.

'**Excuse me, I think I was actually ahead of you in the queue**': You are loathsome and I am inwardly fantasising about your slow and agonising death.

'**No, no, after you**': We are locked in a politeness vortex. This may never end.

'Tea or coffee?': The choice you make will colour my opinion of you, possibly forever.

'Milk, sugar?': Careful now – there is a right and wrong answer to this.

'Milk, no sugar, please': Is the correct answer.

'Two sugars, please': I am a manual labourer.

'I don't drink tea': I am not to be trusted.

'Fond of a drink': Raging alcoholic.

'The odd tipple': I throw gallons of booze down my neck at every available opportunity.

'Eurosceptic politician': Appalling racist.

'Provocative newspaper columnist': Git.

'Conservative MP': Git who went to Eton.

'Doesn't suffer fools gladly': Heartless bastard.

'A bit of a character': Social pariah.

'Did you find the place OK?': We will now have a painfully detailed five-minute conversation about the relative merits of different A roads.

'Ooh, nice': You have just told me where you've been on holiday.

'Ooh, nice': You have just told me where you live.

'Ooh, nice': You have just told me what you had for lunch.

'Ooh, nice': You have just told me your weekend plans.

' … ': You have just unburdened yourself emotionally to me.

'You're looking well': You have obviously been going to the gym, and I sort of hate you for it.

'Out of town shopping centre': Circle of hell.

'High street': Row of betting shops.

'Town centre nightclub': Horrendous meat market.

'Urban redevelopment': We have got a Zizzi now.

'Where do you live?': How expensive is your house?

'What do you do?': How much do you earn?

'New money': Rich person I am jealous of.

'Old money': Rich person I am deferential to.

'Fine': I disagree with what you just said with every fibre of my being.

'Nonsense. Don't mention it': You have wronged me, and I will replay this incident in my head quite possibly forever.

'Mustn't grumble': Will definitely grumble.

'Can't complain': But I'm going to anyway.

'Let's agree to disagree': I loathe you with an intensity that will burn within my soul for all eternity.

'With the greatest respect': I think you're a total moron.

'With all due respect': I disagree with your point of view entirely.

'Let's come back to that': Please do not speak in this meeting again.

'Correct me if I'm wrong': I am absolutely certain I'm correct.

'Sounds good': I wish this didn't sound sarcastic.

'Sounds great': Oh God this sounds even more sarcastic, doesn't it?

'**Yeah, go on then, why not?**': I will be having another drink, if not several.

'**I'm fine**': I am moments away from a devastating mental collapse.

'**I'll bear it in mind**': Let us never mention this again.

'**I'm sure it's my fault**': It's your fault.

'**Not bad, thanks**': I am barely managing to hold back a riptide of emotional agony.

'**Chuffed**': Experiencing heart-racing euphoria.

'**Not too bad, actually**': I think I'm the happiest I've ever been.

'A bit miffed': I have been ripped apart by a tsunami of pain and sorrow.

'Down in the dumps': Severe depressive episode.

'Under the weather': Close to death.

'Gutted': Suicidal.

'Peeved': Consumed with rage.

'Mate': You are very much not my mate, and there is a strong chance I'm about to punch you.

'Mate': I didn't catch your name when we were introduced, and it's too late now to ask.

'Oh dear': A life-altering
catastrophe has just occurred.

'Sorry': You have just trodden on my foot.

'Sorry': You have just bumped into me and caused me to spill an entire tray of drinks.

'Sorry': You have just fallen asleep on the tube and drooled on my shoulder.

'Sorry': You have just smashed into the back of my car.

'You look nice': You have never looked more beautiful.

'Alright you fat wanker, what are you drinking?': You are my best friend and I love you.

British traditions explained

'Blitz spirit': The collective quality of quiet heroism which enables us to withstand calamities such as a tube strike, hosepipe ban or 5 cm of snow.

'Dunkirk spirit': Stoical and good-natured response to flooding, usually involving the stockpiling of sandbags.

'Bank holiday': Three-day drinking binge.

'Public holiday': Excuse for being pissed from lunchtime.

'Christmas day': Excuse for being pissed by 10 a.m.

'Christmas break': Fourteen uninterrupted days of Baileys-soaked indolence.

'Boxing day sales': Zombie apocalypse.

'The bit between Christmas and New Year': Bizarre state of purgatory during which we rehearse for old age by shambling round the house asking each other what day it is.

'What do you make of this weather we've been having?': We have nothing in common, but I'd like to avoid an awkward silence if at all possible.

'**Record-breaking temperatures**': Middling temperatures.

'**Summer time**': Two-week period of collective insanity during which men think it's acceptable to walk down the high street with their shirts off.

'**Would you listen to that rain?**': There is nothing remarkable about this rain, but I'm going to mention it anyway.

'**I think I've caught the sun a bit**': My skin is roughly the colour of an overheating nuclear reactor.

'**Well, we timed this well**': We have made a car journey and experienced only moderate traffic.

'You must come round for dinner': Under no circumstances should you consider this an actual invitation.

'Let's meet up for a drink soon': This will never, ever, *ever* happen.

'Something's come up, I'm afraid': I have decided I can't face an evening in your company after all.

'Dinner party': Excuse for drinking lots of wine and shouting about how good *Breaking Bad* is.

'Would you like a tour of the house?': Our house is worth a lot of money and we would like to show off about it.

'House party': Over-rated event during which acquaintances argue over what to play next on Spotify for four hours, then vomit on the sofa.

'I'm going to Glastonbury': And I'm going to keep banging on about it until you want to karate chop me in the larynx.

'I'm going to Reading and Leeds': I used to be an emo and I can't let it go.

'I'm going to V Festival': I am the star of a second-rate scripted reality show.

'I'm going to Latitude': I am a *Guardian* reader.

'I'm going to Bestival': I am a forty-something former raver.

'I'm going to T in the Park': It's ten days away and I have started drinking already.

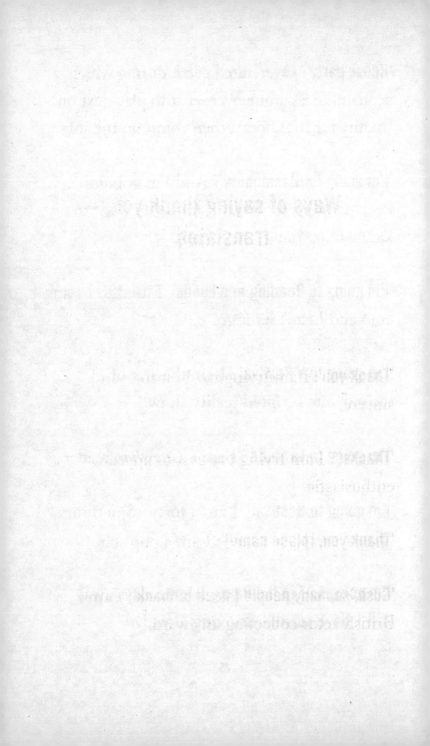

Ways of saying thank you, translated

'**Thank you**': I am trying my best to sound sincere.

'**Thanks!**': I am trying my best to appear enthusiastic.

'**Thank you, [place name]**': I am a pop star.

'**Gosh, so many people I need to thank**': I am a British actor collecting an award.

'I'd like to thank God': I am an American actor collecting an award.

'Ta': I have chosen the laziest possible way of expressing my gratitude.

'Yeah, thanks': I am being sarcastic.

'Thanks a bunch': I am being sarcastic.

'Thanks a million': I am being sarcastic.

'Thanks for that': I am being deeply sarcastic.

'Thanks a lot': I sound sarcastic, even though I don't mean to be.

'Thanks for getting in touch': I am a British office worker.

'Thanks for reaching out': I am an American office worker.

'Thank you so much for the kind gift': You are a distant relative, and decorum compels me to write this bland note.

'Thanks for everything': Dear colleague I don't know very well, this is the best I could come up with for your leaving card.

'Thx': I want you to know I am extremely busy and important, and don't really have time to be writing emails to the likes of you.

'Cheers': I want you to think I'm laid back.

'Cheers!': I want you to think I'm friendly.

'Thanking you': I want you to think I'm a lovable eccentric.

'Nice one, ta': I want you to know I am Northern.

'Many thanks': I am being weirdly formal.

'Much appreciated': I am being weirdly reserved.

'Thank you kindly': I am a top-hat-doffing time traveller from the Victorian era.

'I am forever in your debt': I am a gentleman adventurer from the Elizabethan age.

'Murky buckets': I am wacky.

'Much obliged': I am a London cabbie.

'I owe you one': Please do not consider this a binding contract.

'High five!': I am insufferable.

'Thank you so much': You have done something kind, and I am genuinely grateful.

Greetings:
a translator's guide

'Hey': I like to keep things cool and informal.

'Hey x': I am drunk texting you in the hope of eliciting a mildly flirtatious exchange.

'Hey xx': I am stalking you.

'Hey xxxxxx': I am outside
your flat right now, watching.

'**Hey :-)**': I have instant messaged you, and I can see you're online, so ignoring me will be awkward.

'**Aay**': I am The Fonz.

'**Hey dude**': I am overly friendly, and there is a serious danger that I will insist you high-five me.

'**Hi buddy**': I am an American tourist in London, and will shortly ask you for directions to the M&Ms store.

'**Hello there**': I am devastatingly British, and have at various points in my life seriously considered wearing a monocle.

'**Why, hello there**': I find you attractive, and am raising my eyebrow in the style of Roger Moore.

'Hiya': I am upbeat, to the point of being slightly camp.

'Greetings': I am ruddy-cheeked and avuncular, and am about to slap you quite hard on the back.

'Salutations': I would like nothing more than to be described as 'jovial'.

'Speak': I am a self-important corporate jerk, and this is how I answer the phone.

'Morning!': I am annoyingly chirpy.

'Hullo': I am an Enid Blyton character.

'Ahoy-hoy': I am Alexander Graham Bell.

'Ey up': I am outrageously Northern.

''Ow do': I am outrageously West Country.

'Alreet pet': I am outrageously Geordie.

'Oi oi!': I am a geezer, and will now initiate a loud and obnoxious conversation about tits.

'Weeey': I am drunk, and want you to know I have just attended a football match.

'Wotcha': I am a roguish ducker-and-diver in the style of the Artful Dodger, or possibly Danny Dyer.

'What up': I am a bro.

'Wassup': I think I'm in a Budweiser advert.

'What up my n*a'**: I am white and said this as a joke and now everyone looks horrified.

'Sup': I think I'm a West Coast hip-hop mogul.

'Sup, yo': I think I'm Jesse Pinkman.

'We're done here': I am a middle manager who thinks he's Tony Soprano.

'Blud': I act like a feared member of the criminal underworld, even though I live in Orpington.

'A'ight': I will now attempt to engage you in a complicated fistbump manoeuvre that will end awkwardly for everyone.

'Duuuuuuuude': I am stoned.

'Yo yo yo': I am a douchebag.

'Hii!!!!!!!!': I am a lunatic on the internet.

'**How r u**': I am a weirdo whose friend request you will ignore.

'**What r u wearing**': It's 11 p.m. on a Friday, and this is my slightly tragic attempt at 'sexting'.

'**Hey sexy**': Warning – I am about to send you a picture of my genitals.

'**Dear Sir/Madam, I have been requested by the Nigerian National Petroleum Company to contact you** ...': I am a scammer who mystifyingly still insists on referencing Nigeria, even though by now every internet user on the planet associates Nigeria with scam emails.

'Oh my God you'll never guess what people have been saying about you online': This is a spam link which you will instinctively click on because you are an idiot. The link will then be forwarded to everyone you have ever met, or worked with.

All the ways British men address each other, defined

'Sir': The speaker is required by the terms of his contract to pretend it is a pleasure doing business with you.

'Mate' (1): Is the speaker your actual mate? If so, this is a bit formal. He's about to give you bad news.

'Mate' (2): Is the speaker a stranger? You are about to be punched.

'Chum': You are about to be punched by a UKIP voter.

'Old boy': A UKIP voter is about to ask you to do something.

'Chap': A media executive is about to ask you to do something which you will be required to find charming.

'Squire': You are about to be cheerfully overcharged by 100 per cent.

'Boss': The speaker will tolerate nothing less than immediate payment for the service he is happy to be carrying out for you.

'Chief': Like 'Boss', plus the implication that the speaker is a man of sudden, extreme violence.

'Skipper': Like 'Chief', plus the implication that the speaker has a car boot full of stolen goods at very reasonable prices.

'Guv.': The speaker defers to you in all things, so whatever comes next is really your idea (e.g. sexist joke, institutional racism, systemic fraud).

'My friend' [said in a foreign accent]: You are perfectly safe in this minicab.

'My friend' [said in an English accent]: You have been identified as a dangerous outsider and are being watched.

'Buddy': The speaker wants to borrow something he will never return (e.g. cash, credit for your last fortnight's work).

'Fella': You'd better like football and tits or this is going to end badly.

'Guy': You'd better be interested in house prices or this is going to end badly.

'Geezer': The speaker will tolerate nothing but top bantz from now until the pub closes.

'Pal': The speaker has one fist clenched to hit you, but, worried you might hit back, reserves the right to pretend it's the 1930s and everything's fine.

'Brother': The speaker is stoned or drunk to the point of helpless amity. You are in no danger.

'Bruv': The speaker is stoned or drunk but may turn at any minute. Keep your wits about you.

'Son': The speaker is about to give advice which you both know you'll ignore.

'Lad': The speaker considers you and his sheepdog loyal friends.

'Bro': Are you sure you're in Britain? We don't really use that word ... wait a minute, does the speaker have red trousers and majestic hair? Ah, he just came from Eton. What he means is 'chum' [see above].

'Homie': Like 'Bro', except the speaker left Eton in the 90s and now drives a Mercedes S-class.

'Darling': The speaker went to RADA. Don't expect to get a word in edgeways.

'Blud': The speaker wishes you to know he's got your back in a gun or knife fight. Most commonly said into mobile phones while standing in queues for chocolate milk.

'Cuz': The speaker will be round your house this weekend to take gangsta selfies and watch *Britain's Got Talent*.

'Man': The speaker feels a fuzzy companionship with you as a human being, even if you are currently arresting him.

'Dude': The speaker is trying very hard to sound American, and it's really awkward for everyone concerned.

[Your surname]: The speaker learned personal relations in public school, army or police. You'd better do what he says.

[Your surname with a Y on the end]: The speaker holds you in genuine regard and will gladly hold your pint while you have a slash in a hedge.

[Your first name if it has more than one syllable]: The speaker does not yet know you well enough to shorten your name or assign a new one.

[Your first name with an O on the end]: Your deep and lasting friendship with the speaker depends on neither of you ever doing anything gay together.

'You daft twat': The speaker has no secrets from you, loves you like a brother and at some point tonight will awkwardly man-hug you.

'You c***': Hard to call. Pretty neutral language; a bit over-familiar, maybe. You're probably fine.

Ways of saying goodbye, translated

'Peace out, bra': I am hoping my dreadlocks will blind you to the fact that I'm white and attend a very expensive public school.

'See you on the flipside': I have been watching a lot of 80s buddy movies.

'Live long and prosper': I am a geek. Would you like to see my comic book collection?

'Laters': I am a lad, and have a devastatingly hilarious 'your mum' comeback for every occasion.

'Cheerio': I am a bloody nice chap, and if it were the done thing to wear a bowler hat, I surely would.

'Toodle pip': I think I'm Bertie Wooster.

'Ta-ra': I want you to know that I am more Northern than you. And yes, it is a competition.

'Bye now … yep, bye … bye': I am British, and therefore unable to conclude a phone call without saying goodbye at least seventeen times.

'Adios, amigo': I thought this would sound cool, but I didn't quite pull it off, and now I just feel really self-conscious.

'Ciao': I am an investment banker, and everyone hates me.

'Hasta la vista, baby': I have just made a spectacularly misjudged Arnie reference at the end of a job interview.

Football clichés, and what they really mean

'Dreaded hamstring injury': The second worst thing that can happen to a player, after the 'dreaded metatarsal'.

'There are no easy games in international football': We have just scraped a dismal one–nil victory over the Faroe Islands.

'Derisory offer': We actually received an eye-wateringly huge offer, but the club making it is owned by an oligarch and we think we can screw them for even more money.

'I'm delighted to be here. As soon as I heard of their interest, there was only one place I wanted to go. This is a massive club': I had never given this club a moment's thought until my agent told me how much they were willing to pay me.

'The FA Cup is the greatest Cup competition in the world': This is patently untrue, but we're going to keep saying it.

'Early contender for goal of the season': Moderately impressive half-volley which will be forgotten by next weekend.

'Focus on the league': We have been knocked out of the Cup.

'Focus on the Cup': We have got sod all chance of winning the league.

'Yeah, I was pleased with the goals, but it was all about the team performance today': The victory was entirely down to my individual genius, and we all know it.

'We're just going to take each game at a time and take nothing for granted': As opposed to playing all our remaining fixtures at the same time.

'The lads gave it 110 per cent': Sadly, the other team gave it 200 per cent, and therefore defeated us.

'**We've got to start turning these draws into wins**': I am paid £5 million a year for these devastating strategic insights.

'**Over the moon**': We won.

'**We showed good character**': We lost.

'**In the cold light of day . . .** ': We lost.

'**We gave it everything**': We lost.

'**We did everything but score**': We lost.

'**I thought we were the better team**': We lost.

'**We played some fantastic football**': We lost soooo badly.

'**It's what we do over the season that matters**': We got utterly thrashed.

'**We shouldn't underestimate . . .**': We're playing San Marino in a qualifier and if we don't thrash them it'll be embarrassing.

'**Has a good engine**': Player who runs around the pitch a lot and never scores.

'**For a big lad, he's good with his feet**': Gangly freak who scores a lot of goals.

'**Mercurial winger**': Player who is quite good at making crosses.

'**Wears his heart on his sleeve**': Frequently calls the referee a c***.

'**Half a yard quicker in his head**': Player who is past his prime and should probably retire.

'He'll be disappointed to be beaten from there':
The goalkeeper has just made a mistake so
fist-gnawingly embarrassing his career may
never recover.

**'He'll be gutted not to have scored from that
distance':** A five-year-old would have done
better.

**'He'll be disappointed with that when he sees it
again later':** Confronted with an open goal, a
striker has mystifyingly managed to hoof it
into the stands.

'Speculative shot at goal': Utterly hopeless
thirty-yard toe-punt that almost goes out for
a throw-in.

'They're running the clock down': A player is
shielding the ball, somewhat irritatingly, near
the corner flag.

'Typical striker's tackle': A foul so clumsy it has shattered the recipient's femur.

'They like to get the ball down and play': Which you have to say is a better tactic than leaving the ball constantly floating in mid-air.

'Nobody likes to see that on a football field': A player has done something appalling and quite possibly racist.

'We don't like that in our game': A foreign player has taken a dive, in the exact same way British players have been doing for decades.

'Last throw of the dice': The keeper has run up to the opposition's penalty area, which will make no difference whatsoever.

'Parity restored': Someone has scored an equaliser.

'They'll be partying on the streets of [insert name of city] tonight': A team has won a tournament.

'It was a great ball in, but there was no-one on the end of it': It wasn't a great ball in.

'He's almost hit it too well there': A shot has ballooned dismally over the bar.

'He's found it hard adjusting to the pace of the Premier League': Bafflingly, this lifelong resident of Milan is not all that fond of life in Sunderland.

'The ball quite literally exploded off his foot': Well, not *literally* literally.

'This game needs a goal': We are all so very, very bored.

'David Beckham territory': Any free kick fewer than 35 yards from the goal line.

'Legend': Player who has made more than four appearances for his club.

'Passionate': Player who makes up for his lack of talent by swearing a lot.

'A physical player': Fouls everyone constantly.

'Cultured': Small and foreign.

'Got his feet on the ground': Has not yet been involved in any violent incidents off the pitch.

'Not flashy': Only owns one Lamborghini.

'Local hero': Will sign for a bigger club as soon as his agent can negotiate a high enough fee.

'Sleeping giant': Club with a large following who never win anything.

'Most passionate fans in the country': Scariest fans in the country.

'A man with a lot on his mind': Manager who is about to be sacked.

'Taking each game as it comes': In compliance with the known laws of physics.

'Route one': As distinct from routes two and above, which strangely you never hear about.

'End-to-end stuff': As opposed to a game where the ball remains in the centre circle throughout.

'A game of two halves': As opposed to all those other games with three or more halves.

'The next goal will be crucial': As opposed to all the meaningless goals that have been scored thus far.

'Mazy dribble': A player has run past two defenders in a row before being dispossessed.

'It's like the ball is glued to his feet': A player has dribbled a considerable distance without falling over.

'On paper . . .': What I'm about to say is completely irrelevant.

'At the end of the day . . . ': I am a footballer/manager and I am compelled by some weird hidden law to say this in every interview.

'Go on, my son': Words of encouragement given to superstar player who is not your son, does not care about you, and will soon leave for a more famous club.

'Penalty shoot-out': Guaranteed defeat for England.

'Could this be England's tournament?': This will not be England's tournament.

'A funny old game': It's not remotely funny.

'The beautiful game': The ugly game.

Exceedingly British exclamations

'Bloody hell': I have just been charged £4.90 for a pint, and wish to register my dismay (while nonetheless handing over the cash).

'Blimey': I have just heard the asking price for a one-bedroom flat in south London.

'Bugger': I have just been told I have weeks to live.

'Crikey': I am experiencing intense sexual pleasure.

'Christ': I have sustained a serious injury which requires my immediate hospitalisation.

'Oh for fuck's sake': I have been very slightly inconvenienced by a fellow road user.

'Shit the bed': I have witnessed an exciting moment in a sporting fixture.

'Shitting crikey': I have received news of life-altering significance.

'Jesus titting Christ': I have stubbed my toe, and can't quite believe how much pain I am in.

'Oof': I have witnessed a strong tackle in a football match.

'**Wow**': I wish to convey my amazement at something, but am now worried it may have sounded sarcastic.

'**Christ on a fucking bike**': I have just found out how much more than me a colleague earns.

'**Christ on a fucking pogo stick**': A panelist on *Question Time* has annoyed me, and I am bellowing, purple-faced, at the TV.

'**Yikes**': I have slept through my alarm by an almost imperceptible amount, and will be three minutes late for work.

'**Oh bollocks**': I have a horrible feeling I've just been caught by a speed camera.

'**Fuck it**': I have decided to have a glass of wine anyway, despite it being only 2 p.m.

'Oh fucksticks': I have just been informed of the death of a close friend.

'Oh do fuck off, you fucking wanker': I have just read a troll-y newspaper column specifically designed to enrage someone of my political persuasion.

'FUUUUUUUCK':

I have returned to my car to find a parking
ticket on the windscreen.

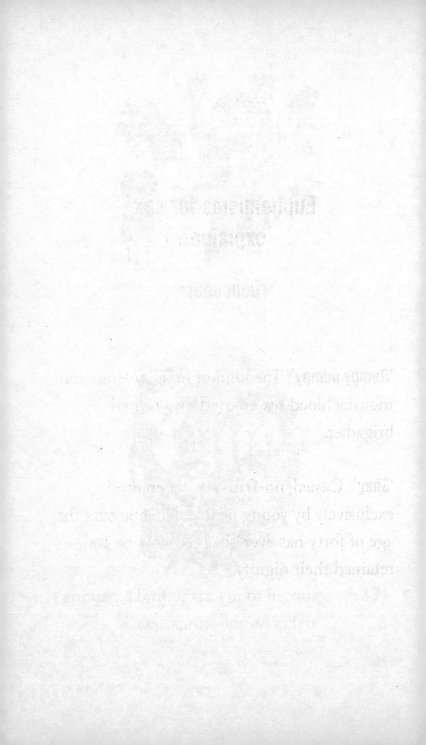

Euphemisms for sex, explained

'Rumpy pumpy': The kind of brisk, solemn and moustachioed sex enjoyed by a retired brigadier.

'Shag': Casual, no-frills sex act enjoyed exclusively by young people. No-one over the age of forty has ever 'shagged' anyone and retained their dignity.

'Romp': Intercourse enjoyed by all famous people, according to the language of tabloid newspapers. Also the kind of sex a businessman might have with his secretary.

'Tryst': Adulterous liaison between two famous people that has been uncovered by a tabloid journalist, usually by means of phone hacking.

'Bonk': Intensely middle class form of sexual congress, during which the words 'Oops' and 'Sorry' feature heavily.

'Knee trembler': Satisfying encounter enjoyed by a Victorian gent, the climax of which very nearly causes his monocle to fall out.

'Banging': The improbably loud sex that your flatmates/neighbours have when you are trying to sleep in on a bank holiday.

'A bit of how's-your-father': Cheeky, end-of-the-pier sex, involving plenty of lascivious winks and Sid James-esque cackling.

'Boning': The kind of sex enjoyed by an American 'bro' during Spring Break. It will be brief but energetic, and he will attempt to high-five you upon completion.

'Slap and tickle': Giggly and innocent encounter, of a sort that last occurred in a B&B in Margate in 1963.

'The beast with two backs': Declamatory, Shakespearean sex.

'Getting jiggy with it': The kind of sex enjoyed by Will Smith.

'Nookie': The kind of sex enjoyed by Fred Durst.

'Hanky panky': The kind of sex enjoyed by Barbara Windsor in the 60s, and Madonna in the 90s.

'Coupling': The kind of sex enjoyed by Gwyneth Paltrow.

'Bumping uglies': The sex that happens in the minds of people who find sex distasteful.

'Humping': The sex that happens when you visit your parents-in-law and their border collie attaches itself to your leg.

'Coitus': Efficient and hygienic sex conducted under laboratory conditions.

'Ménage à trois': Threesome involving a French person.

'Quickie': Form of sex available to parents.

FOOD AND DRINK

Pretentious foodie terms, translated

'Farmer's market': Place where very middle-class people do their shopping to indicate that they are better than you.

'Pop-up restaurant': Establishment where the staff all have tattoos, and you have to queue for hours to get in. Once inside, Instagramming your meal is compulsory.

'**Hot new cocktail place**': Pitch-dark subterranean bar where the drinks are served in jars for absolutely no reason.

'**Hot new eatery**': Place where all the barmen have beards, and the Twitter handle is more prominently displayed than the menu.

'**Artisanal**': Word that once meant 'crafted by hand' but now simply means 'aimed at smug foodies who live in Stoke Newington'.

'**Gastropub**': Establishment that pointedly serves wasabi peas and rice crackers but not crisps.

'**Brasserie**': Like a restaurant but, you know, French.

'Street food': Pulled pork/hot dogs/tacos sold out of an Airstream caravan. Has an air of scuffed authenticity, despite being the second career of a former derivatives trader from Fulham.

'Locally sourced': Sourced from the nearest ASDA.

'Pan-fried': As opposed to fried in a washing machine, or jacuzzi.

'Oven-baked': As opposed to baked inside a car on a hot day.

'Flame-grilled': As opposed to warmed over a Bunsen burner.

'Seared': Because 'barbecued' sounds a bit common.

'Moist': How all cake must be described by law.

'Meltingly tender': How all meat must be described by law.

'Nutty': How all cheese must be described by law.

'Drizzled lovingly': Dolloped.

'Sumptuous': Expensive.

'Enrobed in ...': Smothered in.

'Deconstructed': Mashed up.

'Decadent': Adjective you can apply to a dessert to make you feel like less of a fat bastard for ordering it.

'**Fusion cuisine**': Asian food, but for hipsters.

'**Molecular gastronomy**': Chef waggled a blowtorch at it.

'**Still or sparkling water, Sir?**': *Don't say tap, don't say tap, don't say tap.*

'**Some bread for you, Sir**': That's right, we want you to completely ruin your appetite before eating an expensive meal, because we secretly hate you.

'**Service included**': No need to tip. Unless you are American, in which case knock yourself out.

'Ground pepper, Sir?': I will now produce a pepper grinder so ostentatiously tall as to defy all reason.

'Sommelier': Man in a suit who uncorks your wine in unnecessarily theatrical fashion.

'Master of wine': Person who has spent thousands of pounds studying for this, and will now drone on about 'terroir' and 'mouthfeel' for all eternity.

Crisps, explained

Tyrells: Posh crisps, as indicated by the photo on the pack, which is always black and white and therefore arty.

Kettle Chips: Crisps that were considered posh in the 90s, now thought of as slightly common.

Doritos: Crisps for people who watch *Britain's Got Talent*.

Pombear: Teddy-shaped snack aimed at children and nostalgic simpletons.

Mini Cheddars: Flawless discs of untrammelled joy.

Quavers: Amazingly effete. Basically a cheese-scented sigh in a bag.

Wotsits: Now labelled as 'Baked' in an attempt to be thought of as healthy and wholesome that has fooled absolutely no-one.

Walkers: Solid and utilitarian, their chief purpose is to serve as the Platonic ideal form of the crisp.

Walkers Sensations: The party crisp. Because you can't serve regular Walkers to guests, lest they think you poor.

Monster Munch: Snack that you will enjoy in the moment but will leave you troubled by a sense of ineffable, oniony melancholy for many hours afterwards.

Pringles: Known to mathematicians as an example of a hyperbolic paraboloid. Known to the rest of us as, 'ARGH TAKE THESE BLOODY THINGS AWAY FROM ME'.

Things people say in pubs, vs. what they mean

'**The usual**': The fact I am able to say this and be understood is one of my proudest achievements, despite being evidence of a crippling alcohol dependency.

'**Just a half for me, thanks**': I will be back to order the second half in approximately forty-seven seconds.

'A pint of ... that one, please': This guest ale has a quirky name and I'm too self-conscious to say the words 'Hoptimus Prime' out loud.

'White wine spritzer' : I get drunk easily, and believe a weaker drink will delay the point at which I start shouting/weeping/accusing the barmaid of being a 'slag'.

'Lager and lime': I am feeling adventurous.

'Stella': I am feeling fighty.

'Foster's': I am driving, and believe drinking a beer that is 1 per cent weaker will make all the difference.

'Gin and slimline tonic': I am feeling virtuous.

'Large whisky, straight': I am feeling melancholy.

'Vodka tonic': I am doing Dry January, and this doesn't count as booze, right?

'Double vodka and Red Bull': I am going clubbing.

'WKD': I am a twenty-something male, and there is a strong chance I will attempt to engage you in 'banter' at some point.

'Just nipping out for a fag': It's my round.

'Just going to the bar, can I buy anyone a drink?': Though there are a couple of people on this table I don't know very well, so when I say 'anyone' …

'OK, it's my round': Offer STRICTLY limited to pints or wine, nothing 'fancy'.

'Oh go on then, if you're having one': I deliberated for all of one picosecond.

'One more for the road': And then probably several more in front of the *Graham Norton Show* when I get home.

'I really shouldn't': But I obviously will.

'It's OK, I don't need a tray':

The ability to carry four pints without spilling a drop is the only man-skill I have ever mastered. Please allow me this rare chance to demonstrate it.

'Large glass, or small?': Go on, pretend to mull this over.

'Just a coke for me, please': I am either pregnant, or a recovering alcoholic.

'Six pints of Stella, two glasses of Pinot Grigio, a pint of Pimms, and I can I pay on card, please': I am the world's worst person, and everyone behind me in the queue has every reason to despise me.

'Wide selection of craft beers': Baffling array of drinks you have never heard of, and cannot distinguish between.

'Guest ale': Unpopular beer we over-ordered and are now trying to get rid of.

'Real English pub': Full of Real English alcoholics.

'Traditional pub food': Chips, chips, chips and more chips.

'Bar snacks': Otherwise known as 'dinner'.

'Scampi Fries': Eye-wateringly pungent snack which has somehow avoided being classified as a biological hazard.

'Pork scratchings': Because a night of heavy drinking wasn't already unhealthy enough.

'Packet of crisps': Snack that you will be required to 'open out' to the entire table, even if it means consuming precisely two each.

'Local pub': Dismal place you would stop going to if only you could be bothered to walk three minutes further from the office.

'Family pub': Annoying children welcome.

'Sourz, four shots for £5': Under-age drinkers welcome.

'Make it a double for £1 extra': Piss-heads welcome.

'Beer garden': Three-square-foot area of concrete.

'Happy hour': Invitation to quickly get very drunk immediately after work.

'Open mic night every Tuesday': Be sure to avoid this pub on Tuesdays.

'Regular': Solitary drinker whose inexorable slide into chronic alcoholism is acknowledged with good cheer by all.

'Greetings, stout yeoman of the bar': I am a UKIP supporter.

Wetherspoons: Establishment whose hideousness you will overlook because YAY, RELATIVELY INEXPENSIVE BOOZE.

Walkabout: Cheerless hangar in which twelve different sporting fixtures are playing on giant screens simultaneously and no-one speaks.

'Pub lunch': We will drink four pints, shamble back to work and then fall asleep at our desks.

'Time at the bar, ladies and gentlemen':
Will you fuck off now, please.

'You don't have to go home but you can't stay here': Seriously, though, please fuck off.

'If you could just make your way outside, gents, that would be much appreciated':
Fuckofffuckofffuckofffuckoff.

Things you order in a cafe, translated

Latte: I am a busy urbanite and therefore crave the energising jolt of an enormous cup of warm milk.

Cappuccino: I don't really like coffee, but can't bring myself to admit it.

Espresso: I actually find this drink acrid and unpleasant, but believe ordering it gives me a suave, George Clooney-ish quality.

Double espresso: I enjoy the sensation of eye-bulging, heart-racing panic first thing in the morning.

Americano: I am aware this is just an ordinary coffee, and am secretly annoyed that I am required to order it by this special name every time.

Mocha: What I really want is a hot chocolate.

Gingerbread latte: What I really want is a pudding.

Flat white: I am not entirely sure how this is different to a latte, if at all, but I understand that it is the edgy, modern thing to order.

Long black: The drink I would prefer, but I can't order it because I'm worried it might sound slightly suggestive.

Macchiato: Whatever this is, I'm confident that ordering it will make me appear sophisticated and continental.

Chai latte: I am an earth-mother type who advocates hypnobirthing, and probably walks around the house naked a lot.

Babyccino: I will sit here all day with my shrieking toddler because this is what mums do. Also the wi-fi is free.

Fruit tea: I am so insanely health-obsessed I have managed to convince myself that a cup of scalding, lemon-scented water is preferable to a caffeine fix.

Fruit booster: I am willing to pay £2.60 for a small amount of fruit juice with ice because I am absolutely demented.

'Tall': I am aware this is actually your smallest size, and find your quirky naming system irritating, but will reluctantly go along with it for the sake of being polite.

'Grande': I am hungover and require coronary-inducing levels of caffeine before I can show my face at work.

'Venti': Please give me the maximum amount of coffee allowable by law.

Danish pastry: I crave sweetness.

Baguette: I crave cheese.

Panini: I crave disappointment.

Muffin: Yes, I am eating cake for breakfast, and I am not ashamed.

Large salted caramel hot chocolate with extra cream and marshmallows: I have quite simply run out of fucks to give.

Condiments, explained

Horseradish: Deceptively potent sauce, ideal for enhancing a delicious roast dinner with the sensation of your head being engulfed in flames.

Wasabi: The same, but for Japanese people and hipsters.

English mustard: Substance which, when consumed in even the tiniest quantities, has the power to make your eyes stream and your throat to close, very much like a chemical weapon.

Dijon mustard: Benign variety enjoyed by effete continental types. Does not cause sweating, nausea or facial flushing, and is therefore not a real man's mustard.

Brown sauce: What's in it? Nobody knows. Just 33 cl of lovely, lovely brown.

Tomato ketchup: 96 per cent delicious splodge. 4 per cent evil watery bit with the power to utterly ruin your meal/day/life.

Salt: Bewitching murder dust. Negative – causes high blood pressure which can lead to heart disease or stroke. Positive – makes chips taste nice.

Worcestershire sauce: Supposedly good for 'zhushing up' cottage pie or chilli, though it's primary value is as an ingredient in a Bloody Mary, the only socially acceptable way to drink vodka before lunch.

Mayonnaise: All-purpose gloop. Definitely the condiment to go for if you want your food to have that all important 'nothingy' quality.

Salsa: The only condiment so exciting as to inspire a lascivious, snake-hipped style of dance. No-one goes to brown sauce classes, which in itself is telling.

Lime pickle: Curry house punishment. Tests show that not one person has ever spooned lime pickle on to a poppadum until all three other dips have been exhausted, including the stupid salad one, which isn't even really a dip.

Deciphering wine labels

'Crammed with jammy red fruit': Red.

'Bursting with aniseed and vanilla on the finish': Red.

'Hints of damson and burnt toast': Red.

'Bold': Red.

'Floral top notes': White.

'Hints of citrus': White.

'A powerful nose of ripe pear, caramel and candied lemon': White.

'A full-bodied explosion of tropical fruit': White.

'Notes of pear drops and Palma Violets': White and fizzy.

'Biscuity': Champagne.

'Excellent supermarket wine in the sub-£10 bracket': This is the only review you will read.

'Robust': Gets you drunk.

'Easy drinker': Gets you drunk quickly.

'Powerful and complex': Gets you completely smashed.

'**Fruit forward**': Posh way of saying fruity.

'**Will age well for several years**': But you will drink it immediately anyway.

'**Ready for drinking now, but could benefit from being laid down for a few more years**': Hahahahahaha. Yeah. Good one.

'**Biodynamic**': Aimed at pretentious people.

'**Mineral-driven**': Tastes of ... wine.

'**Luxurious mouthfeel**': Tastes all right.

'**Concentrated and intense while maintaining its elegance**': Tastes nice.

'**An appealing array of flavours and aromas**': Tastes really nice.

'Approachable': Not like those wines that make you run away screaming.

'Excellent structure': Not like those wines that evaporate the second you turn your back on them.

'Perfect for barbecues': As opposed to being swigged on a park bench at 9 a.m.

'Affordable': The only adjective you give a shit about.

RELATIONSHIPS

Online Dating:
a user's guide

'**I'm on OKCupid**': I am bland.

'**I'm on Match.com**': I am desperate.

'**I'm on Guardian Soulmates**': I am agonisingly middle-class.

'**I'm on Grindr**': I am gay. And I'm staring at you right now, from across the bar.

'I'm on Tinder' [male]: I am a compulsive masturbator.

'I'm on Tinder' [female]: I am not looking for a date. I just enjoy laughing at douchebags.

'I'm on all of the above': I have literally no standards anymore.

'Looking for fun': Looking for sex.

'Looking to make friends': Friends I can have sex with.

'Looking for my knight in shining armour': Looking for someone who is good at sex.

'No-strings': No conversation. Just sex.

'Up for a laugh': Up for some sex.

'Down for whatever': So desperate for sex you wouldn't believe.

'Looking for someone who's active': No fatsoes, please.

'No baggage, please': I am heartless.

'I don't take life too seriously': I am mindless.

'Outdoorsy': I went camping once.

'Adrenaline junkie': I cycle to work.

'Fitness fanatic': Ten minutes on the cross-trainer.

'Marathon runner': Marathon bore.

'Homebody': Loner.

'Hobbies include . . .': Things I pretend to enjoy include . . .

'Extreme sports': I once owned a skateboard.

'Yoga': I went to a Bikram class, and fainted.

'Literature': Anything by Dan Brown.

'Theatre': Does *Grease: The Musical* count?

'Video games': I live with my parents.'

'World of Warcraft': I am a virgin.

'Curling up on the sofa and watching a DVD': I have no hobbies or interests to speak of.

'Staying in and watching telly':

While weeping.

'Hanging out with friends': At least I would, if they weren't all married now.

'I like cosying up in front of the fire': One day I hope to live somewhere that has a fire.

'I'm a fun active girl who likes to hang out with her friends and watch movies': I had no idea what to write in this box. Will this do?

'The odd glass of wine': Gallons of wine.

'I like walks in the park': I am a human being with legs.

'I love to travel': I am a human being with a passport.

'Family is really important to me': I am a human being with parents.

'I'm terrible at talking about myself': And yet I've just written 1200 words in the 'About Me' section.

'What you see is what you get': I really couldn't be arsed filling this bit out.

'I love shows like *Breaking Bad*, *The Wire*, *True Detective*': But not as much as I love *Snog, Marry, Avoid*.

'Looks are not important to me': Though if you are under six feet tall you can get lost.

'I am six feet tall': I am not, but I'm hoping you'll have forgotten I said this by the time we meet.

'Tall, dark, handsome': One of the three, anyway.

'Loving life': Lonely.

'Independent': So, so lonely.

'My life is fab, I just need someone to share it with': I am desperately, suicidally lonely.

'I work hard, play hard': I am a massive twat.

'Hello, ladies': Please kill me.

'My friends say I'm . . .': In my dreams I'm . . .

'Fun loving': Obnoxious.

'Bubbly': Cretinous.

'The life and soul': Voice like a foghorn.

'Quirky': Tiresome.

'Laid-back': Boring.

'Down to earth': Really boring.

'Cuddly': Obese.

'Hedonist': Drug addict.

'Genuine guy': Dangerous fantasist.

'GSOH': I tell abysmal jokes.

'I love to laugh!': I am a simpleton.

'I'm a glass-half-full kind of person': I am basically Forrest Gump.

'I don't watch television': I am pretentious.

'I'm here for some good banter': I am appalling.

'I'm not looking for anything serious': I have been planning my wedding day since I was nine years old.

'Really nice guy': I will fashion a suit from your skin and wear it round the house.

Getting married:
a handy phrasebook

'Stag do': Dismaying foreign jaunt which will ruin you financially, swallow several days of your holiday allowance and force you to bond with strangers with names like Bazza, Dazza and Wazza.

'Hen do': Marathon drinking binge during which you will be expected to loudly discuss sex toys with an enormous number of people you don't really know that well.

'Wedding': Test of endurance during which you find out which members of your extended family are able to drink Prosecco for ten hours straight without falling over or starting a fight.

'Wedding list': Mercenary list of demands by two people who are already wealthy enough to afford a £20,000 wedding.

'Wedding DJ': Person whose iPod contains 'Come On, Eileen', 'Brown Eyed Girl', and, in the event of requests from the mums, Michael Bublé's entire back catalogue.

'Best man': Person whose otherwise touching and heartfelt speech will be marred by a climactic volley of ill-advised dick jokes.

'Groom's speech': Opportunity for the groom to say all the beautiful and moving things he found when he panic-Googled 'Groom speech tips' two days ago.

'First dance': Awkward, self-conscious shuffle during which the couple profoundly regrets choosing the twelve-minute extended version of 'Bat Out Of Hell'.

'Wedding night': Occasion upon which sex must occur, no matter how paralytic both parties are.

'Honeymoon': Two-week festival of smugness, sun cream and near-constant shagging.

'Pre-nuptial agreement': Important legal document indicating a complete absence of trust between two parties.

What married people say, vs. what they mean

'I'm going away on business': I am having regular drunken regrettable sex with someone at work.

'You're my rock': You are cold, grey and inscrutable.

'Happy Valentine's!': You like enforced public displays of affection, right?

'**I fancy a cosy night in**': I can't be bothered to go out.

'**Shall we get an early night?**': Let's read our phones in bed for an hour before falling asleep.

'**I'll cook you a special anniversary meal**': M&S are doing Dine In for £10 at the moment.

'Why are you looking at me like that?': Oh tits, I've forgotten our anniversary, haven't I?

'I've bought you some flowers': I have been unfaithful.

'I've bought you a spa treatment': I have been unfaithful.

'I've bought you a puppy': I have been spectacularly unfaithful.

'I've bought you a car': I have been unfaithful repeatedly for twenty years

'Date night': Drunk night.

'Romantic meal for two': Pizza Express on Orange Wednesdays.

'Camping holiday': Annual jamboree of disillusionment, poor sanitation and mutual recrimination.

'Oh, you don't have to get me anything for Christmas': But if you don't I will cut you.

'I don't want a big fuss made out of my birthday': Under NO circumstances should you take this literally.

'You shouldn't have': I wish you hadn't.

'I'm fine' [male]: I am OK.

'I'm fine' [female]: I am barely managing to hold back a tidal wave of hormonal rage.

'Will you marry me?': I'm thirty-four. You'll do.

'The man of my dreams': The man I've settled for.

'For richer, for poorer': Though hopefully mostly richer.

'In sickness and in health': Unless you contract an STD.

'Till death us do part': Well this is depressing.

Break-up lies,
exposed

'**I've been thinking**': Prepare for the worst.

'**We never talk any more**': You talk, but I don't listen.

'**I'm not happy**': Well, I am sometimes. Just not when I'm with you.

'**We need to talk**': It's curtains, dickwad.

'You deserve better': I deserve better.

'You're too good for me': Yes, I'm dumping you, but also kind of giving you a compliment, so if anything you should be thanking me.

'We're too alike': You're too boring.

'I need some time out': During which I can sleep with other people.

'I need time to get my head together': I need to have sex with someone else.

'I just need some space': I just need to sleep around a bit.

'I'm not ready to settle down': I haven't had enough casual sex yet.

'I think we should see other people': I think I should see other people.

'I'm scared of commitment': I think I can do better.

'I'm just not ready for a relationship right now': And yet, ironically, I will start dating someone else within forty-eight hours.

'Whoever ends up with you is so lucky': The poor bastard.

'I think we should take a break': Preferably a permanent one.

'I'm just such a mess right now': I am dumping you, but also trying to elicit some sympathy. It's pretty audacious when you think about it.

'If anything I like you too much': I am just flat-out lying.

'I really need to focus on work': I am having sex with someone at work.

'I love you like a friend': But not that friend I'm shagging. A friend I don't fancy.

'I wish things had worked out between us': I wish I could dump you by text and not have to have this conversation.

'I don't want to hold you back': You're holding me back.

'We're just at different points in our lives': I am way out in front.

'My feelings for you are so intense they scare me': I have absolutely no feelings for you.

'I do love you. I'm just not in love with you':
I don't love you.

'It's not you, it's me': It's definitely you.

'There's no-one else involved': Not one person,
no. Loads of people.

Things parents say, vs. what they mean

'Don't worry, we won't let becoming parents destroy our social life': Dear all our friends without children: goodbye. We'll see you again in eighteen years.

'NCT class': Opportunity for parents-to-be to hear horror stories from shell-shocked veterans.

'The miracle of childbirth': Fourteen-hour period during which a normally reserved and cheerful woman transforms into the demon girl from *The Exorcist*.

'It wasn't the easiest of births': I spent several days bellowing myself hoarse at anyone who came near me.

'Of course, I foreswore all pain relief and had a purely natural birth': Whereas you had an epidural which means you're WEAK and I am better than you.

'Thanks for the baby name suggestions, we'll certainly keep them in mind': FFS, we're not calling it 'Zuul', OK?

'Of course, as the father I wanted to play my part too': I did absolutely sod all other than make a 'soothing' iPod playlist featuring that Snow Patrol song you quite like.

'Mother and baby doing fine': Baby doing fine. Mother absolutely knackered, to be honest.

'A healthy baby girl, 7.5 pounds': Look, we know you don't give a toss how much it weighs, but we have to tell you, it's tradition.

'Baby monitor': Chagrin-generator.

'Muslin': Vomit-sponge.

'Moses basket': Vomit-collector.

'Having kids is the greatest thing that have ever happened to me': OH GOD, PLEASE HELP ME I'M SO TIRED.

THE MEDIA

Today on Radio 4 ...
those listings in full

Today Programme: John Humphrys says something cantankerous, Evan Davies says something cheery, followed by an item about failings in social care services, and now here's Gary with the sport.

Thought For The Day: A Bishop mentions something that's been in the news and then makes an incredibly tenuous link with a passage from Leviticus.

In Our Time: Top academics conduct an incredibly erudite discussion about string theory. Three minutes before the end you will realise you haven't listened to a single word and have learned precisely nothing.

The Shipping Forecast: Item which has no function in the modern age, but which can never be dropped from the schedules for fear of middle class people firebombing the BBC.

Desert Island Discs: A bizarrely reverent interview with a celebrity chef who will discuss his deep and abiding love of Bach's cantatas, while failing to mention at any point his fondness for the works of B*Witched.

Farming Today: Early morning show we are only doing because the charter says we have to, though no-one is listening so this could be an hour of slide-whistle and fart noises for all you care.

Woman's Hour: A harrowing report on female genital mutilation in Sudan, followed immediately by a light-hearted item on shoes.

Afternoon Drama: Painfully worthy portrayal of the hardships faced by clog-manufacturing single mothers in Indonesia.

The Archers: The sound of crunching gravel, interspersed with an awful lot of sighing.

Just a Minute: Panel show that has lost its edge of late but you remember as being quite funny in its heyday, i.e. around 1882.

Front Row: A slightly pompous newspaper columnist and a theatre impresario review a film that has just come out, which you will sort of half-listen to while chopping an onion.

Book At Bedtime: Serialisation of a novel that has had really good reviews and you would love to stick with it if only you could zzzzzzz.

Magazine headlines, translated

'**Exclusive interview**': Not remotely exclusive, but we can't just put the word 'interview' on the cover, it'd sound weird.

'**Unrivalled access**': We were allowed on the tour bus for a bit.

'**Reveals all**': Reveals sod all.

'On the road with . . .': We watched a gig, then interviewed the band backstage.

'Her most honest interview yet': We had twenty minutes in a hotel room, and she gave us the exact same quotes she gave everyone else.

'He says, flashing a smile as he stands to leave . . .': It didn't happen like this, but I need to give this article a satisfying ending, and this is the only way I know how.

'12 steps to a flat stomach': Top tip: eat less.

'The ultimate abs workout': That'll be some sit-ups, then.

'New year, new you': New year, exact same article.

'Get a ripped torso in 12 days!':

You will buy this magazine, leaf through it on the train home, and then immediately consume five cans of Skol and a Zinger Tower Burger.

'10 steps to mindblowing sex': Yes, it's that article about Kegel exercises again.

'Jen's New Heartache': We'll stop printing this guff when you people stop buying it.

'Brangelina Bombshell': Ludicrous fiction designed to distract you from the futility of your existence for a few fleeting, shame-filled moments.

'What men really want in bed': Hint: blowjobs.

'The sex issue': Our publisher said we needed to sell some actual magazines this month.

'Special get-back-in-shape issue': The follow-up to our 'fuck it, let yourself go' issue.

'Men's magazine': A famous woman in her pants, some aftershave ads and an article by A.A. Gill that no-one will read.

'Women's magazine': 165 pages of fashion and beauty, plus a random article about Syria near the back in a bid to appear classy.

'Gossip magazine': Blatant nonsense about reality TV stars, which you will flip through in a daze while hungover.

'Fitness special': There will be a diagram illustrating how to do a pull-up.

'Sunday newspaper': Made up of eighty-five sections, eighty-three of which you will take a strange delight in immediately hurling in the bin.

'Sunday supplement': Brochure full of things you cannot afford, seemingly designed to make you feel depressed and inadequate.

The news, decoded

'The BBC has learned ...': According to a rival news source that we're not going to credit ...

'It has emerged': We read it in a newspaper.

'A source said': I will now pad this article out with an entirely made-up quote.

'North London-based celebrity': Jewish celebrity.

'Intensely private Hollywood star': Actor who is gay and famously litigious.

'Much-loved 1970s television personality': Predatory paedophile.

'Veteran entertainer': Sex offender.

'Lothario': Sleeps with anything that moves.

'Ladies' man': Bit rapey.

'Post-match interview': How many clichés can this sportsman reel off in three minutes?

'Famously outspoken star': Lairy buffoon.

'Selfie': A celebrity has taken a picture.

'On a day of fast-moving developments': This story is dull, and we are trying our best to liven it up.

'Gaffe': Minor slip-up by a politician which we will not shut up about until he or she has resigned.

'Slammed': Criticised.

'Hit back at': Replied.

'Frenzied knife attack': As opposed to a calm and gentle one.

'High-speed car chase': As opposed to a slow one.

'Full-scale riot': As distinct from a half-riot.

'Fierce gun battle': As opposed to a quiet, soothing one.

'Tragic death': As opposed to dying for the LOLs.

'Raft of measures': As opposed to a Viking longboat of measures.

'Brutal murder': As opposed to one of those nice, friendly murders.

'Storm': Mild controversy, mostly whipped up by us.

'Went viral': Someone retweeted something.

'Holed up for crunch talks': Some men in suits are at a conference.

'Tributes pour in': We will now copy-paste some tweets about a dead person.

'The rain failed to dampen people's spirits':

It pissed it down and everyone
was miserable.

'Displaying impressive confidence, Prince George has taken it all in his stride': Baby behaves in baby-like fashion.

'In what could turn out to be a defining moment': Or it could not.

'Killer storms to ravage Britain': Expect a stiff breeze.

'Viewers took to social media to express their disapproval': Here comes a list of tweets.

'Declined to comment': We didn't bother asking for a comment.

'Would neither confirm nor deny': Did not answer our emails.

'My cocaine shame': Famous person takes drugs.

'My cocaine hell': Famous person has a memoir to plug.

'Heroin, bagels, kidnapping and me': Sensationalist cover line linking three words that cropped up randomly during the interview.

'Romp': A famous person had sex.

'Trysts': A politician had sex.

'Influx of migrants': Load of old bollocks in the *Daily Mail*.

'Maddie disappearance clues surface': Load of old bollocks in the *Sun*.

'Diana death exclusive': Load of old bollocks in the *Daily Express*.

'BIG BRO HEIDI SEX PIC SHOCK':
Load of old bollocks in the *Daily Star*.

'The unpalatable truth about quinoa':
Load of old bollocks in the *Guardian*.

'Crater that looks like Susan Boyle found on the moon': Load of old bollocks in the *Sunday Sport*.

Today's TV highlights

Newsnight: A succession of oleaginous guests dodge every question, before an incongruously wacky bit at the end where Kirsty Wark does the worm to 'Get Lucky' as the credits roll.

Question Time: A widely loathed right-wing MEP, an obscure backbencher and the chief political correspondent of the *Daily Telegraph* get together and say things like 'Let me be clear' and 'We're getting away from the real issue here', while everyone at home tweets about how awful it is.

Britain's Got Talent: This week – some breakdancing sixth formers, a window cleaner who thinks he's Ed Sheeran and a Labrador that can do the cha-cha-cha.

The X Factor: 70 per cent contestants' back stories soundtracked by Coldplay and designed to manipulate your emotions, 20 per cent recaps, 8 per cent *Carmina Burana*, 2 per cent actual singing.

Gogglebox: 'Reality show' that captures real families watching telly, though curiously we never see them do what people actually do in front of the TV, which is to stare at their phones before falling asleep.

Strictly Come Dancing: Bright lights, trumpets, Brucie tells a lame joke, an orange-skinned man in high-waisted trousers rhumbas with a female newsreader, and everyone at home thinks, 'They have got to be shagging.'

The Andrew Marr Show: A man who resembles the Crazy Frog flaps his arms about before being joined by Harriet Harman for a discussion about reducing net migration.

Countryfile: This week's highlight – an interview with a man in a Barbour jacket who is concerned about a slight decline in Shropshire's water vole population.

Jeremy Kyle: Typically fraught episode, in which a lie detector test helps settle that all-important question: Did Chantelle get pregnant by a bloke called Darren while she was going out with another bloke called Darren?

The Graham Norton Show: A Hollywood actor is joined on the sofa by a soap star she clearly hasn't heard of, and laughs uneasily at wanking jokes she doesn't quite understand.

Rude Tube: Show aimed at people who enjoy watching videos on YouTube, but find themselves thinking, 'If only these clips were bookended by inane links by Alex Zane.'

Made In Chelsea: Will the blandly attractive posh woman finally get together with the blandly attractive posh man? You'll just have to wait and see.

Homes Under The Hammer: Daytime TV show that is only ever watched through a veil of tears, by those who are either unemployed, sick or depressed.

Mock The Week: More biting political satirical observations, such as 'Eric Pickles is fat'.

Escape To The Country: Property show in which a stratospherically wealthy couple look bored, sour and unimpressed while they are shown round a succession of palatial residences.

Countdown: Programme which you have watched religiously for years purely in the hope that one day the anagram might one day spell out PISSFLAPS.

The weather forecast, translated

'Further rain across central areas': That's your bank holiday plans fucked, then.

'Southern parts becoming murky overnight': Sleep soundly in the knowledge that tomorrow will be utterly miserable.

'Severe weather warning': This is your cue to book the day off work, panic buy everything in Tesco, and worry hysterically about Britain's stockpiles of gritting salt, before waking up to light drizzle and a stiff breeze.

'Extreme snow alert': There will be a fine dusting of snow, which will inexplicably cause the entire national transport network to collapse.

'Flood warnings': As we speak, BBC news reporters are wading down high streets, ready to deliver pieces to camera where they have to shout dramatically over the wind.

'Northeast, backing northwest later, 4 or 5': You have no idea what this means but it sounds nice, doesn't it?

'Rockall, Malin, Hebrides. Rain, then squally showers. Poor, becoming moderate': Hush now, Britain. Shhhh, sleepy time.

'A pulse of heavy rain will push west across central/southern Scotland': Just in case you were expecting sweltering heat and sand storms.

'Cloudy across central parts with occasional rain or drizzle': So good luck with that garden party you planned, suckers.

'Cloudy with a chance of sunshine': There is absolutely no chance of sunshine.

'Sunny spells expected throughout the day . . .': The Pogues' 'Fiesta' plays, entire population runs outside to stock up on Piz Buin and Pimms.

'Amid scattered showers': Population tuts, walks back indoors, slumps in front of *Masterchef*.

'Rain, occasionally heavy': From now until the end of time.

Celebrity Gossip, exposed

'Flaunts her curves': Woman wears clothes.

'Pours her curves into ...': Woman wears dress.

'Exposes her toned mid-riff': Woman wears bikini.

'Shows off her pert derrière': Woman has backside.

'Leaves nothing to the imagination': Woman has breasts.

'Bevy': Collective noun for beauties.

'Cut a lonely figure': We cropped the other person out of the picture.

'Steps out in a VERY revealing dress': We've capitalised the word 'very' to indicate we sort of disapprove, but still want you to look at the photos.

'Suns herself on the beach': Having first tipped off several photo agencies as to her whereabouts.

'Looked visibly upset': Our photo editor picked out the one shot where she looked upset.

'Looked drawn and haggard': When we hid behind a bin and photographed her leaving the house to buy milk at 6 a.m.

What advertisements say, vs. what they mean

'Back 2 School': Shop sign with the power to trigger a plangent sense of sorrow, even though you are thirty-four years old.

'Boxing day sales': Zombie apocalypse.

'Get on down to Homebase': Go ahead, waste your bank holiday.

'I'm lovin' it': Enjoy a few moments of furtive, greasy bliss followed by hours of bloating and self-recrimination.

'Just Do It': Tell yourself you'll do it, buy some expensive trainers to enable you to do it, but somehow never quite get round to doing it.

'New formula': Desperate bid to reverse nose-diving sales.

'One of your five a day': Inches you closer to reaching an arbitrary and meaningless target.

'Velvet quilted toilet tissue': Won't make your bumhole sore.

'Ultra-absorbent': Capable of mopping up all bodily fluids, even the really disgusting ones.

'Natural': Not actively poisonous to human beings, as far as we're aware.

'Organic': Mystifyingly expensive.

'Probiotic': Sugary yoghurt drink.

'Gluten free': Aimed at gullible hypochondriacs.

'Friendly bacteria': You need these to be healthy. Shut up, yes you do.

'A source of Vitamin D3': You have no idea if that's a good thing. Better buy it anyway.

'Herbal supplement': Crock of shit.

'25 per cent more effective!': There is no way of testing this claim.

'For a limited time only': Available until people stop buying it.

'Superfood': Unremarkable food stuff for which there is a baffling and faddish enthusiasm.

'Antioxidant serum': Snake oil.

'Now with added plant sterols!': Don't even pretend you know what that means.

'Clinically proven': We paid a man in a lab coat to approve this.

'Fructifying extracts': Yes, we think you're stupid enough to believe that fruit makes your hair shiny.

'Super-firm hold grooming putty': Hair gel.

'Extreme styling paste': Hair gel for estate agents.

'Sculpting clay': Hair gel for twats.

'Hydra energetic X-treme moisturiser for men': A beauty product, yes, but not one that will make you look gay.

'Turbo booster face wash': Nope. Not remotely effeminate.

'Maximum hydrator': You strapping heterosexual goliath of a man, you.

'Energising power scrub': Just to reiterate: not gay.

'Naturally pure and balanced spring water': Exactly the same as what comes out of the tap but you'll buy it because you're an idiot.

'Natural ingredients': Such as sodium laureth sulfate, dimethicone, disodium cocoamphodiacetate, glycol stereate.

'Low in fat': Stuffed with sugar.

'Enjoy as part of a balanced diet': We're looking at you, lard-arse.

'Here comes the science bit': Here comes the spurious bollocks bit.

'Scientists agree': In a study we funded.

'Hypoallergenic': A word that has no medical meaning whatsoever, but no-one seems to have noticed.

'Peptidique': Vaguely French and sciencey sounding word we just made up.

'Hydrolysed microprotein nutricomplexes': Literally mashing random words together now.

'Ultra-rich protective lotion': Moisturiser.

'Advanced skin corrector': Moisturiser.

'Multi-lift anti-wrinkle night cream': Moisturiser.

'Radiance regenerating serum': Moisturiser.

'Enriched youth-activating concentrate': Look, it's all the same bloody stuff, OK?

'Energy drink': Heart attack in a can.

'Diet drink': Diabetes in a can.

'No-frills air travel': Dehumanising ordeal.

'Honest banking': We'll initially rip you off a fraction less than our competitors will, then make it up with baffling extra fees later.

'Drink responsibly': Yeah, right.

'Enjoy responsibly': Drink just enough so that karaoke sounds like a good idea, but not so much that you text your ex.

'Packed with vitamins and minerals': And a shit ton of sugar.

'A family business': Owned by a rapacious multi-national corporate giant.

'Honest, no-nonsense grub': We're a subsidiary of a huge conglomerate but we think you won't notice because our packaging features a cool font and a picture of a penguin.

'We understand our customers': We patronize you with adverts featuring larky, non-threatening bearded men and ukulele music.

'Payday loan': We will lend you money at a crippling interest rate.

'The company of the future': Our CEO thinks he's Steve Jobs.

'Committed to sustainability': Our CEO drives a Prius.

'Committed to efficiency': Our CEO wants to sack everyone.

'Making the world a better place': We spent millions on a pompous TV ad soundtracked by Sigur Rós.

'**Global ambition**': We made a corporate video featuring the following elements: a wise-looking old man in indigenous garb, time-lapse footage of motorway traffic by night, a newborn baby, a graduate throwing her mortar board into the air, and beaming children from an evenly representative mix of races.

'**Wrinkles appear reduced**': Appear reduced. Not actually reduced.

'**The great taste your cat will love**': Like he gives a shit. This is a creature that will happily tear the head off a vole.

'**Gourmet food for dogs**': Basically ringpieces and entrails, but we got Joanna Lumley to voice the ad and jacked up the price.

'100 per cent real beef': May contain traces of horse.

'Handmade on a farm in Devon': Then processed and vacuum-sealed in a factory in China.

'From our value range': Handpicked for scum like you.

'We're not like other companies': We are exactly like every other company.

The internet:
a translator's guide

#Hashtagging #every #word #in #a #sentence:
I don't understand what hashtags are, so I use
them on everything to be on the safe side.

Writing. Full. Stops. After. Every. Word:
I am overly dramatic.

'A thing I wrote . . .': I am a journalist and am
pretending to be off-hand about an article
that I am secretly extremely pleased with.

'Thrilled to announce': I have got a new job and I demand praise.

'Smart take': I am a serious person sharing serious articles.

'Another wonderful column by @caitlinmoran': I am sucking up to a celebrity in the deluded hope of a follow.

'LOL': I am entirely stony faced as I type this on my phone while queuing up at the Post Office.

'RIP :-(': I am tweeting the news of a celebrity death in a shameless bid to win retweets.

'YOLO': I have just done something incredibly pedestrian and unremarkable.

'Just sayin': I didn't know how to end this tweet. Will this do?

'OMG': I am excitable.

'ZOMG': I am zany.

'OMGGGG': I am irritating.

'WTF': I am confused.

'FFS': I am angry.

'FTW': I am impressed.

'Amazing': I am easily impressed.

'UH-MA-ZING': I am a simpleton.

'Amazeballs': For some reason I adopt the vocabulary of a five-year-old whenever I go on the internet.

'Two more sleeps until ...': I expect you to find my use of language kooky and eccentric.

'Nom nom nom': I am about to eat some delicious food. Also, I am a cretin.

'Totes': I live in West London.

'OMG so random': I don't know what random means.

'I can't even': I think I'm in *Clueless*.

'On the interwebs': I am too wacky to just say 'internet'.

'This wins the internet': Here is a moderately amusing YouTube clip featuring a dog on a surfboard.

'Meh': I am a joyless person who refuses to be impressed by anything.

'I just spat my tea out/snorted tea through my nose!': I didn't, but I want you to know I found this amusing.

'I just ran 10k in 47 minutes with Fitbit': It's not enough for me to feel healthy. I need you to feel guilty about being less healthy than me.

'Just completed a 4.03 mile run with #runkeeper': I also scarfed down an entire sharing bag of Doritos while watching *Take Me Out*, but I'm not willing to share that.

'Amazing weekend. Feeling so blessed to have so many wonderful friends': Not like you. Your friends are rubbish and all your weekends are miserable.

'Thanks for all the birthday messages!': Important reminder to anyone who hasn't yet acknowledged my birthday – this is your last chance. And yes, I will notice if you don't.

'Can't believe so-called friends would stoop so low': I am deliberately leaving a vague Facebook status in the hope that people will give me some attention and ask what happened.

'Come on you Spurs!!!!': I realise most of you are not watching this match and will be baffled by this update, but I simply don't care.

'Cheeky selfie with my besties': God I'm wonderful. Admit it, you'd kill to be me.

'Losing love is like a window in your heart ... ': Lyrics from a song that I am currently listening to, and somewhat arrogantly assume will resonate with you as well.

'26 miles done. Still just about in one piece!': Meanwhile you're still in bed, hungover, scrolling glumly through Facebook. I pity you.

'Two and a half years ago today we welcomed our little angel into the world': I think I am the first man in the history of the world ever to father offspring.

'Josh just did his first grown-up poo! So proud': I am so utterly lacking in self-awareness I expect you to find this cute.

'Daddy's little soldier sleeping soundly. #awwww': He's been an absolute little git all day.

'After sex #selfie': I am an appalling human being.

'Nightclub #selfie': Look at me.

'Bus stop #selfie': Look at me.

'Brushing my teeth #selfie': Look at me.

'Taking a selfie #selfie': Look at me.

'Taking the recycling out #selfie': LOOK AT ME.

Newspaper site comments, decrypted

'**How is this news?**': This article was not interesting to me personally, therefore it should not exist.

'**Did you get paid to write this?**': I disagreed with this article, and have decided to be a dick about it.

'**I expect more from you**': I have never paid to read anything on this website, yet I nevertheless believe you owe me something, rather than the other way round.

'You do realise there's a war in Syria, right?':
I don't believe that a news website should
write about more than one thing at a time.

'That's five minutes of my life I'll never get back':
My time is precious. So precious that I spend
hours a day leaving douchey comments on
the internet.

'Wake up, sheeple!': I see conspiracy theories
everywhere, because it makes my existence
seem less tragically insignificant.

**'David SCAMeron, leader of this Con-Dem-Nation,
is no better than the loathsome Tony BLiar and his
cronies':** That's right, I'm making laboured
puns out of people's names. Take that,
establishment.

'I'm just sick to death of gay people ramming their lifestyle down our throats': I am a retired, married man who spends an awful lot of time thinking about gay sex.

'I'm not racist but . . .': I am about to say something eye-wateringly racist.

'A disgrace. This is why I am leaving the country': There is absolutely zero chance of my ever leaving the country.

'It's a disgrace how these foreigners swamp our borders and never bother to integrate into British society': Writes Barry, who lives in Malaga and has never once attempted to integrate into Spanish society.

'We need to clamp down on all these scroungers who get benefits and contribute nothing to society': Writes Judith, who draws a state pension and keeps getting life-saving operations free on the NHS.

'Speaking as an honest, hardworking member of society . . .': Who nonetheless spends most of the day in his dressing down, masturbating angrily and arguing on the internet.

'We need to stand up for British values': By being relentlessly grumpy about absolutely everything that happens here.

'I am absolutely furious. Fuck you all': I am a bit lonely, and really all I want is some attention.

CRITICS

Books

'Must-read': You really don't need to read it.

'Page-turner': Book with lots of short sentences, designed to be read by people who don't read much.

'Gripping': A book in which something exciting happens.

'Poignant': A book in which something sad happens.

'**Rollicking**': A book in which something amusing happens.

'**Sweeping**': A book that has more than three-hundred pages.

'**Gritty**': A book featuring poor people.

'**Chilling**': Generic ghost story.

'**Taut**': Generic thriller.

'**Startlingly original**': Arty novel that critics will rave about and no-one will buy.

'**Unflinching**': 'Real-life' misery memoir, the majority of which is almost certainly made up.

'Tear-jerking memoir':

Your mum will read this in the bath.

'Provocative': Non-fiction book that will inspire a tedious opinion piece on 'Comment is free'.

'A tale of loss and redemption': Forgettable airport novel.

'A writer at the height of his/her powers': Successful writer churns out more of the same.

'Winner of the Man Booker Prize': Worthy novel that you will tell people you enjoyed even though secretly you found it a chore.

'Laugh-out-loud funny': Guaranteed to be the exact opposite.

'Tour de force': I enjoyed this book, but I can't think of anything to say about it.

'Agatha Christie meets Dan Brown meets Lionel Shriver': And now for a few comparisons to pad out the review.

'At once compelling, haunting and mysterious': I'll be honest, I'm just trying to reach the word count now.

'Chick-lit at its finest': Book with a pink, sparkly cover featuring a line drawing of some shopping bags.

'Fast-paced, intricate thriller': Book with a silhouetted man, presumably a spy, on the cover, designed to be read by holidaying dads.

'Sprawling fantasy epic': Overlong book with a man wielding a sword on the cover, aimed at *Game Of Thrones* fans/virgins.

'Blood-suckingly good vampire fiction': Book designed to look exactly like the *Twilight* books, in a bid to trick old people into buying it for teenage relatives.

'Sizzling erotica': Shameless *Fifty Shades of Grey* rip-off.

'I couldn't put it down': One day I might actually read it.

'Hilarious page-turner': Cynical cash-in trotted out by a Sunday newspaper columnist in about three weeks.

'The next *Gone Girl'*: The publishers desperately want this to sell as many copies as *Gone Girl*.

TV

'Hangover TV': Any programme shown on a Saturday morning.

'Guilty pleasure TV': Any programme shown on a Saturday evening.

'Post-pub TV': Porno channel that makes money by encouraging drunk masturbators to make premium-rate phone calls.

'Sunday night drama': Gentle, soporific detective show designed to be half-watched by your mum and dad while they leaf through the *Daily Mail*.

'Cult Scandinavian drama': Incredibly slow-moving and complex show that you keep falling asleep in the middle of, but persevere with in case you are called upon to discuss it at a dinner party.

'Talent show': Show in which zero talent is on display.

'Scripted reality show': Cheaply made TV series featuring posh, good-looking young people being weirdly awkward and stilted with each other.

'Late-night current affairs programme':
Panel discussion show featuring a pompous right-wing newspaper columnist, and angry lefty firebrand and an obscure Lib Dem MP who begins every sentence by saying, 'Let me be clear.'

'The best show since *The Wire*': American TV series that you don't really want to watch but so many people have recommended you end up buying the box set just to shut them up.

'The best show since *Breaking Bad*':
Humourless and depressing drama that literally everyone will be banging on about for the next year, so you might as well just give in and watch it.

'Radio 4 comedy': Genuinely the least amusing thing you will ever hear in your life.

Music

'Their finest album yet': We say this every time.

'Achingly beautiful': The singer does a lot of falsetto.

'Banger': Moronic dance track that will be A-listed by Radio 1.

'Glacial': Sounds a bit like Sigur Rós.

'A return to form': Achingly average album by a veteran musician that we are being nice about in a bid to secure an interview.

'Like [X] on acid': Has psychedelic bits.

'Like [X] on speed': Has fast bits.

'Like [X] on downers': Has slow bits.

'Like [X] on heroin': Has really slow bits.

'Legendary producer': Person who you have never heard of.

'Epic': Any song lasting longer than six minutes.

'Seminal': Album appreciated exclusively by *Mojo* journalists.

'The next big thing': Quite similar to the old thing.

'Mercury Prize winner': Artist who you will see on *Later ... With Jools Holland* and subsequently never hear of again.

'The next Mumford And Sons': Maddeningly twee indie band featuring an extravagantly bearded banjo player.

Film

'Explosive thriller': Features plenty of hot sex and explosions.

'Masterpiece': Self-consciously 'dark' superhero film that dumb people will consider to be really intelligent.

'Summer blockbuster': Sequel.

'The event movie of the year': Characters from one comic book franchise meet characters from another comic book franchise.

'White-knuckle thrill-ride': Godawful action movie starring Jason Statham.

'The film everyone's talking about': And by everyone, we mean film critics.

'Noirish': No-one beyond *Time Out* and Mark Kermode will give a shit.

'Steamy': You will be able to masturbate to this.

AT WORK

What people say in the office, vs. what they mean

'Breakout session': We will sit in a room and repeat very dull ideas.

'As a team we need to move out of our individual siloes': We all hate each other.

'Let's action this': I don't understand the difference between nouns and verbs.

'I'll inbox you': I am a bit of a twat.

'**Let's take this offline**': I am a massive twat.

'**It's been great working with you guys, and I'll really miss this team**': So long, suckers.

'**CC**': I am passive aggressively alerting as many senior people as possible to your fuck-up.

[On the phone] 'Could you put this in an email?': Which I will ignore.

'**I'm going freelance**': I miss daytime TV.

'**I'm an SEO expert**': I know how to put keywords in a headline.

'**I'm an analytics expert**': I have got a Google Analytics log-in.

'**I'm a social media expert**': I am a bullshitter.

'Ninja': Douchebag.

'Community manager': Person who writes the tweets.

'It's time for a fresh challenge': I literally couldn't stand being in the same room as you a day longer.

'I can't wait to get started!': I actually can, but everyone has to say this, right?

'I'm taking a career break': I will be sitting in my pants watching *Jeremy Kyle* and crying for the next three months.

'I've been offered a fantastic opportunity elsewhere': I have been offered more money elsewhere.

'Quick pint after work':

Several pints after work, and quite possibly
some shots too.

'Company away day': Must we?

'I know how to code': I know how to italicise things in HTML.

'Let's park this for now': Let's never mention this ever again.

'Welcome to the company, lovely to meet you!': Get promoted above me and I will cut you.

'I'm an experienced manager': I bought a book from WHSmith on being a manager.

'I'm working from home today': I am not doing any work today.

'I've got the lurgy': I am hungover.

'I've got man flu': I am hungover.

'I've got a doctor's appointment':
I am hungover.

'Happy Birthday!': We've never spoken. Why
am I signing this?

'Pub after work? Can't, I've got plans I'm afraid':
I have spent quite enough time with you
people for one day.

'Anyone fancy a cup of tea?': Offer strictly
limited to the three people in my immediate
vicinity.

'Nipping to the shops, anyone want anything?':
Within reason. I'm not your fucking
dogsbody.

'What are you eating there? Looks nice': I am on
the 5:2 diet and I'm so hungry and miserable
I could scream.

'**Cycled to work, eh? Good for you**': You smug bastard.

'**I want more responsibility**': I want a pay rise.

'**I'm giving a presentation**': I have put some boring graphs together in Powerpoint.

'**In my last company . . .**': What I'm about to say is totally irrelevant.

'**Team player**': Has basic social skills, is not an outright sociopath.

'**This is beyond my remit**': I can't be arsed to deal with this.

'**He's certainly ambitious**': He's appalling.

'**It's been a pleasure working with you**': I have forgotten you already.

'How's the wife?': I have forgotten your wife's name.

'How are the kids?': I have forgotten your kids' names.

'How are things at home?': I have forgotten everything about you.

'How was your weekend?': It's Monday or Tuesday.

'What are you up to this weekend?': It's Thursday or Friday.

' … ': It's Wednesday.

'Come intern for us': Come work for us for no money indefinitely. It's illegal but hey.

'He's intensely results-driven': He's a psycho.

'Doesn't suffer fools gladly': Merciless bastard.

'He's the office entertainer': Total wanker.

'She'll go far': She's terrifying.

'He's straight-talking': Every other word is fuck.

'Best wishes': I am dying inside.

'Regards': This job is slowly killing me.

'Xxxxx': I am overly affectionate.

'XOX': I am zany.

':-)': I am childish.

'x': I typed this by mistake. Awkward.

'Cheers!': I hate you!

'Yours': Up yours.

'Kind regards': Go fuck yourself.

What bosses say, vs. what they mean

'We wish [X] the best of luck in her new job': Burn in hell, traitor.

'Our model is scalable': The company will either grow, or it'll shrink. One of the two.

'Skyrocketing revenues': Negligible profits.

'Sharp uptick': Tiny, almost imperceptible increase.

'We are tax efficient': We avoid paying tax.

'I've decided to step down': I have been given a massive payoff.

'We just had different visions for where the company was going': They found out I'd been embezzling funds.

'Moving on to pastures new': Fired.

'We're restructuring the company': Everyone is fired.

'We've brought in a team of consultants': Everyone is about to be fired.

'You're fired': I think I'm Alan Sugar.

'By mutual agreement ...': The boss thinks ...

'In this brainstorm, there are no bad ideas': This brainstorm will be nothing but bad ideas.

'Got time for a chat?': Prepare for the worst.

'Can I have a word?': We will have many, many, many, many, many words.

'Can I have a quick word?': I don't have anything to discuss, I just like putting the fear of God into you.

'Have you got a minute?': You've got a minute.

'We need to develop a more agile workflow': We should probably stop titting about on Facebook all day.

'Merger': Excuse to fire everybody.

'Following the restructuring, [X] will be taking on some additional responsibilities': We have chosen our fall guy and have set them up to take all the blame for our fuckups.

'MORNING TEAM!':

Everyone hates me.

'Exciting new position': It isn't an exciting position.

'I've been recently reading the biography of Steve Jobs': I am not Steve Jobs, and never will be.

'Core values': Making money.

'This is a really great opportunity for our business': We are sooooooooo screwed.

'I don't think there's ever been a more exciting time to be working in this field': We are sooooooooooo soooooooooooooooooo screwed.

'The Chinese symbol for "crisis" is a combination of the symbols for "danger" and "opportunity"': We are more profoundly screwed than you will ever believe.

'**We should run this past legal**': We should have someone else to blame in case this goes tits up.

'**It's been a challenging year**':
We are totally fucked.

'**We're seeking new revenue streams**':
We are broke.

'**We're restructuring our financing**':
We are broke but not ready to admit it.

'**The economic outlook is uncertain**':
The economic outlook is apocalyptic.

'**The company is perfectly positioned to meet the tough economic challenges ahead**':
The end is nigh.

'**It's been a great year**': For our shareholders.

'The success we've had is down to every single one of you': We are all getting bonuses. You're not.

'The door to my office is always open': I wish facilities would bloody fix it.

'I'll take your ideas on board': I'll steal your ideas and take credit for them.

Popular fonts, decoded

Arial: I am boring.

Georgia: I am unimaginative.

Didact Gothic: I am pretentious.

Gothic Pro: I am condescending.

Times New Roman: I haven't changed the default settings on Word yet.

Verdana: I fancy a change, but nothing too dramatic. I wouldn't want to upset anyone.

Narrow: I'm being sarcastic.

Courier New: I'm feeling classy.

Demi Bold: I am feeling shouty.

Impact: I am feeling very shouty.

Ultra Light: I am feeling enigmatic.

Comic Sans: I am a dangerous lunatic who deserves to be shunned.

MODERN LIFE
IS RUBBISH

What estate agents say, vs what they mean

'Early viewing recommended': It's already gone.

'An exciting opportunity has arisen': In shock news, we have a house available.

'Up-and-coming area': Might not be horrible in a decade's time.

'Increasingly popular area': Horrible, but lots of people are as desperate as you.

'Popular area': You can't afford to live here.

'Sought-after location': Only Russian oligarchs can afford to live here.

'Borders on [X]': Don't tell people you live in [X] if you ever want them to find your house.

'Deceptively spacious': Not spacious.

'Cosy': Really not spacious.

'Perfectly sized': Humans can barely fit in this.

'Bijou': Humans cannot fit in this.

'Compact': Cats cannot fit in this.

'Charming': Doesn't have stairs.

'Quaint': Doesn't have windows.

'Rustic': Doesn't have a roof.

'Authentic': Is made of mud and straw.

'Easy access into the city': It's not in the city

'An extensive range of shopping facilities nearby': There's a Tesco Metro, a newsagents and a laundrette you'll never use.

'A substantial double-fronted detached house': It is a detached house.

'An exceptional period conversion flat': It is an old flat.

'A well-presented two double bedroom maisonette': It is an expensive flat so we're trying to make this sound classy.

'Superb lounge': It has a lounge.

'It has a wonderful flowing entertaining space': I am basically just talking crap now.

'Fully-fitted kitchen': Good news, you won't need to provide your own sink.

'WC/bathroom': There's a toilet, but we call it a WC because it makes it sound slightly more upmarket than using the word 'toilet'.

'The development is located minutes away from this incredible city attraction': You will visit the attraction twice, even though you can see it every time you sit on the WC/toilet.

'The flat has an open day': You will have less than an hour to purchase this house, otherwise it will be gone forever and your dreams will lie in ruins.

'Well presented': They hoovered before you arrived.

'Superbly presented': They stuck some daffodils in a jug too.

'A building full of character': It was designed by MC Escher and decorated by a psychopath.

'A building with a lot of history': Look at this dent, look at this dent, look at this dent, is that a bloodstain?

'This apartment has heating and carpets fitted': We are running out of stuff to say about this flat, so I am just listing stuff you normally find in a house.

'Key deposit': Give us money.

'Reservation fee': Give us money.

'Administration paperwork fee': Give us £100 to do some photocopying or you're homeless.

'This area's got a village-like atmosphere': Your mugger knows your name.

'There's a real sense of community': You know the junkies' names.

'Plenty of amenities': Your corner shop has a cashpoint.

'Good transport links': There's a bus stop ten minutes' walk away.

'One bedroom flat': I am a billionaire.

'Studio flat': Bedsit.

'Studio flat': Cupboard.

'Studio flat': A box where loneliness is your only friend.

'Studio flat': Ahahahahahaha I hate you.

'Studio flat': Look at me driving round in my shiny branded company car, bet I earn more in a month than you'll earn all year, in your FACE loser.

'Split-level studio flat': There's a bunk bed.

'Mezzanine sleeping area': Shelf with a mattress.

'Aspirational living': We are ripping you off.

'Riverside living': We didn't say which river.

'Waterfront apartment': We think that's water in the canal.

'Must be seen': May not actually exist.

'Recommended viewing': The pictures are horrible, aren't they?

'New price': Over-priced last time.

'Reasonable offers considered': We are getting desperate.

'Priced to sell': I am getting sacked if this doesn't sell.

'Boasts': Has.

'Benefits from': Has.

'Comprises of': Has.

'Convenient for local amenities': Inconvenient for everything else.

'Easy to maintain': It won't take long for you to vacuum the ten square feet of floor.

'Great use of space': No idea how they managed to fit a bed in there.

'Three bedrooms': Two bedrooms and someone can sleep in the kitchen.

'Original features': Nothing has ever been repaired.

'Strong potential': Spend £100,000 on repairs and it might be habitable.

'Would benefit from': For some reason does not yet have.

'Needs modernisation': Good luck if you expected plumbing.

'Great scope for improvement': Like, you could add walls.

'The opportunity to make this your own': LOL there isn't actually a building at all.

'Elegantly proportioned': All the rooms are as small as each other.

'Full of character': Full of mice.

'Ideal for first-time buyers': Hahaha suckers.

'Would suit': This is not for the likes of you.

'Garden flat': Basically a dungeon with some moss on a paving slab outside.

'Minimalist': Basically a hollow shell.

'Modernist': The walls are at right angles.

'Neoclassical': No idea what this means but it sounds fancy.

'Art deco': Nope, not a clue.

'Rococo': We just like the sound of this.

'Bauhaus': I have got one of their albums somewhere.

'Well appointed': Yeah, we're just saying random words now.

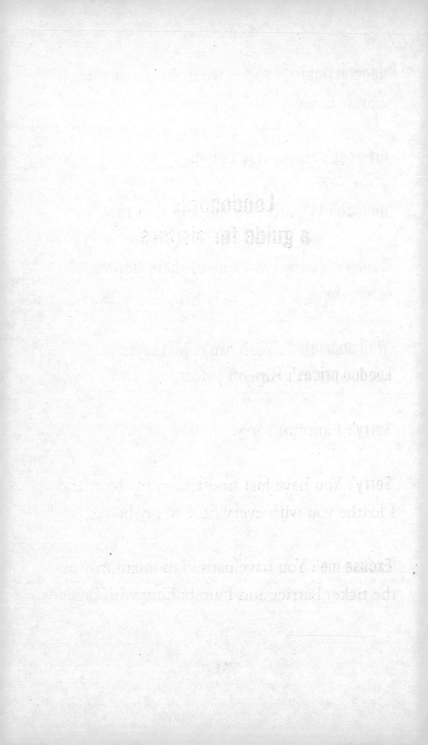

Londoners:
a guide for visitors

'London prices': Rip-off prices.

'Sorry': I am not sorry.

'Sorry': You have just trodden on my foot, and I loathe you with every fibre of my being.

'Excuse me': You have paused momentarily at the ticket barrier and I am boiling with rage.

'My fault entirely': Your fault entirely.

'I'm fine, thanks': I am barely managing to conceal a churning maelstrom of emotions.

'How are you?': Fine. Just say fine.

'See you Saturday!': Don't forget to email me twice to make sure that we're actually meeting on Saturday.

'Let's have lunch': Let's walk to Pret and back as fast as we can.

'I'm having a party in Wimbledon, come along': Please travel for four and a half hours as I live in the middle of bloody nowhere.

'Open for business': Oligarchs welcome.

'Centre of global finance': Money launderers' paradise.

'My commute? It's not too bad. About average': It involves three modes of transport, takes hours each day, and is slowly crushing my spirit.

'Could you move down a bit please?': I am not asking, I'm telling.

'Could you move down a bit please?': I am seconds away from a devastating mental collapse.

'Could you move down a bit please?': If you don't, I will start killing indiscriminately.

'Due to adverse weather conditions': It was a bit windy earlier.

'Due to the wet weather conditions':
A tiny amount of rain has fallen.

'Please take care when ...': Don't you dare
blame us if ...

'We apologise for the inconvenience caused': Via
the medium of this dehumanised pre-
recorded message.

'Due to a signalling failure ...':
Due to an excuse we just made up ...

'Rail replacement bus service':
Slow, agonising descent into madness.

**'There is a good service on all London
Underground lines'**: Though this very much
depends how you define 'good'.

'Planned engineering works':
That's your weekend plans fucked, then.

'Would Inspector Sands please report to the operations room immediately': Ohgodohgod everybody panic, we're all about to die.

'Annual fare increase': We are rinsing you suckers for even more money. Again.

'House party in Tooting? See you there!':
South of the river? No fucking chance.

'I live in Zone One': I am unimaginably wealthy.

'The area is really up and coming': Only one tramp shouts at me in the morning.

'Vibrant': Actual poor people live here.

'Gentrification': I am so glad they're rid of the poor people.

'Gentrified': Oh bollocks now I can't afford to live here either.

'Efficient use of space': Microscopic.

'Incredible potential': Absolute shithole.

'Affordable': Uninhabitable.

'Authentic': Fake.

'I just bought a flat': My parents just helped me buy a flat.

'Swift half': Many, many, many, many halves.

'Quick pint': In the pub until closing time.

'We're going on a date': We're getting pissed together.

'Picnic': Daytime piss-up.

'Barbecue': Piss-up in the garden.

'South London': Here be monsters.

'West London': Here be posh people.

'East London': Here be young people.

'North London': Here be newspaper columnists.

'Oxford Circus': Roiling hellscape.

'Tech city': Bunch of startups you've never heard of.

'London has some of the best restaurants in the world': So how come I always end up at Nandos?

'London is full of cultural delights': Which I never visit.

'Gourmet coffee': Ludicrously overpriced coffee.

'Exciting pop-up restaurant': You guys like queuing, right?

'We have a no bookings policy': We hate our customers.

'This pub has character': This is not a gastropub, and I'm scared.

'Traditional boozer': Pub that does not serve wasabi peas.

'**He works in finance**': He's a psycho.

'**He works in media**': He'a a wanker.

'**He works in PR**': He's a bullshitter.

'**He works in tech**': He's got a blog.

'**Working hours**': Waking hours.

'**Greatest city on earth**': Apart from New York.

'**You know what they say: He who is tired of London . . .**': I am so tired of London.

Politics, unspun

'Let me be clear': I think this makes me sound authoritative.

'Let me be absolutely clear': I think this makes me sound trustworthy.

'Let me be absolutely open and honest': No-one believes a word I say.

'What I'm hearing on the doorstep is . . .': What I've just read on Twitter is …

'If you'll just let me finish': If you'll just let me steamroller right over you.

'I hear what you're saying': And I'm going to disregard it.

'To get back, if I may, to the point I was making': Shut it, oik.

'The dire situation we inherited from the previous administration': Don't blame us if the country's fucked.

'There is no instant solution': We have no idea how to fix this.

'It's going to take time': Don't hold your breath.

'There are no easy answers': We haven't got a clue.

'Our message is very clear and very simple':
[Followed immediately by something that makes no sense whatsoever]

'We want to see a wide range of options right across the board': I am buying time while I think of an answer to this question.

'That is why we're putting in more money in real terms than any previous administration': Christ, I hope no-one actually checks this.

'The one per cent': The zero point zero zero one per cent.

'Wealth creators': Swiss bank account holders.

'Looking at a comprehensive raft of measures': Doing absolutely fuck all.

'We had a robust exchange of views':
We openly despise each other.

'Allegations made in a Sunday newspaper':
Juicy sex scandal.

'I would like to apologise for errors of judgement': I was papped snorting mephedrone with a rent boy.

'These press reports are unfounded and the minister has my full support': We have already drafted the poor bastard's resignation statement.

'The PM has assured me I have his full support': Oh balls, I'm going to have to resign, aren't I?

'The minister has dedicated her life to serving her party, country and constituency': She's a goner.

'We thank the minister for her many years of distinguished public service': Byeeee.

'Parliamentary expense': Second home in Wimbledon.

'Wide-ranging independent inquiry': We're kicking this into the long grass.

[Incomprehensible, bovine parliamentary jeering]: I couldn't agree more.

[Incomprehensible, bovine parliamentary jeering]: I disagree strongly.

'I refer the right honourable gentlemen to the answer I gave some moments ago': Go fuck yourself.

'We stand together shoulder to shoulder': For the purposes of this awkward photo call.

'Metropolitan elite': The BBC.

'Special relationship': Sucking up to America.

'Market forces': Companies that donate to our party.

'Britain is open for business': Britain welcomes dodgy oligarchs.

'We have reached a historic trade agreement with China': By not once mentioning their human rights record.

'A firm commitment to cutting emissions': Which we have punted down the road another few years.

'Climate change is happening now': But we're still not going to do anything about it.

'Further incursions will be met with all appropriate force': Friendly reminder that our military is bigger than yours.

'He's a man of integrity': No major scandals yet.

'He's a man of the people': Didn't go to Eton.

'She connects with voters': Appeals to the lowest common denominator.

'It's time for a change': Vote for me.

'It's time for a new beginning': Please vote for me.

'It's time for real leadership': OH GOD JUST VOTE FOR ME YOU WANKERS.

'The squeezed middle': Waitrose customers.

'Hardworking families': Tesco customers.

'The less well off': Poundland customers.

'The most vulnerable members of our society': Lidl customers.

'Alarm clock Britain': People who wake up in the morning.

'Austerity Britain': Excuse to make all the cuts we were going to make anyway.

'In these straitened times': Better get used to being poor.

'Return to growth': Return to an ever-so-slightly slower rate of decline.

'The Big Society': OK, we give up, sort it out amongst yourselves.

'We're all in this together': LOL.

What celebrities say, vs what they mean

'This new album is my most honest work yet':
It's exactly the same as all my other albums.

'It features a real mix of styles': It's all over the place.

'It has a contemporary feel': It features a supremely ill-advised dubstep bit.

'I feel I've matured as an artist': This album has a ballad on it.

'As a songwriter ...': As someone who employs an army of songwriters ...

'We'd like to play some new material for you now': Please don't go to the bar.

'You guys are honestly the best crowd we've played to on this entire tour!': Where are we again?

'Thank you, and good night!': I will now stand backstage pointlessly for five minutes while you half-heartedly bellow for more because those are the rules god damn it.

'I contemplated suicide': I didn't, but I realise you need a pull-quote for this article and I'm happy to oblige.

'If I'd carried on that lifestyle, I'd be dead right now': I was drinking as many as two, three glasses of wine a day.

'I hit rock bottom': I woke up with a hangover.

'I'm clean and sober': I have cut out the booze. It's just crystal meth now.

'I'm just enjoying being single right now': I am gay.

'I guess I just haven't met the right woman yet': I am very, very, very gay.

'I don't like to comment on my private life': I am so gay it's not even funny.

'I'm getting married!': People of the press, meet my new beard.

'I struggle with my body image':
I have a workout DVD coming out.

'I'm actually a real homebody': At least I would
be if I wasn't out taking MDMA every night.

'I hate glitzy celebrity parties': Unless there's a
chance I'll be papped, in which case count
me in.

**'My job is nowhere near as glamorous as people
think':** It's still more glamorous than yours,
though.

'I'm an intensely private person': My self-worth
is entirely predicated on being worshipped by
strangers.

'I'm not someone who craves validation': Love
me, love me, love me, love me, love me.

'Fame is not important to me': I would decapitate my own mother for a BAFTA.

'I don't like to share every little detail about myself': I only tweet thirty times a day.

'I'm not really a Twitter person': I pay a PR firm to do all that for me.

'I resent media intrusion into my private life': Apart from when I have something to plug.

'I try not to read what people say about me online': I get a Google alert every time someone mentions my name.

'My work is popular with real people, not so-called critics': My work is exclusively enjoyed by morons.

'The allegations against me are outrageous, vicious and completely false': But I've hired some incredibly expensive lawyers, just to be on the safe side.

'I intend to fight to clear my name': I will settle out of court, and hope this all goes away.

'I've long been a fan of the amazing work this charity does': I could do with some good press.

'I thought it was time to give something back': My publicist thinks this will make people hate me less.

'I am running a marathon to raise money for ...': I mean, I could just make a donation, but that wouldn't generate any publicity, would it?

'**I work incredibly hard**': Several days a week, in fact.

'**Working with Brian on this film was a dream come true**': He said if I mention the sex stuff I'll never work in this town again.

'**Working on this film has been the most rewarding professional experience of my life**': I got paid sooooo much money.

'**This role was incredibly demanding physically**': For my body double.

'**I underwent a complete physical transformation**': I put on some weight, then lost it again.

'**Yes, we've heard the rumours, but I can assure you we're just good friends**': We have not stopped boning since the day we met.

'It's a real departure for me': It's going to bomb, isn't it?

'It's a labour of love': Turkey alert.

'It's a quirky ensemble piece': Literally no-one will care.

'It was well received at Sundance': It's insufferably pretentious.

'It's a screwball comedy': It's as funny as bowel cancer.

'It's a historical drama': It's long, tedious and will win an Oscar.

'It stars Vince Vaughn': It's atrocious.

'It stars Jennifer Aniston': It will go straight to DVD.

'In real life I'm actually quite dull': My life is an endless whirligig of adulation, debauchery and pleasure. But no-one wants to hear that, do they?

'I'm not flashy': Last year I spent £5 million on drugs and pillows.

'I'm not as rich as people think': I earned more money while giving this interview than you'll earn all year.

'I come from a working-class background': Daddy could barely afford the RADA fees.

'I don't think of myself as a sex symbol': As long as everyone else thinks of me as a sex symbol.

'You should see me without make-up first thing in the morning': You will never, ever, ever see me without make-up.

'I believe a woman should age naturally':
My face is so paralysed by botox I am no
longer capable of expressing human emotion.

'This might surprise people, but I eat junk food all the time': And then throw it all up immediately afterwards.

'I'm trying a new diet regime': I regularly starve myself almost to the point of organ failure.

'I hate going to the gym': Which is why Claudio, my personal trainer, visits me privately.

'I can honestly say I'm happier now than I've ever been': I hate myself and want to die.

Acknowledgements

Thanks to Simon Lewis, Tom Phillips and Scott Bryan for the inspiration; Scott Lamb and Ben Smith at BuzzFeed for giving me a job that I love (and enables me to write the kind of nonsense that makes up this book); and my colleagues at BuzzFeed UK for being lovely, brilliant and making me laugh every day.

You can find me on Twitter here: @lukelewis #quickpintafterwork